PENGUIN BOOKS

JAPAN-THINK, AMERI-THINK

Robert J. Collins, born and educated in the United States, has pursued a professional business career in Tokyo since 1977. During this time he has also served as chairman of an international school board and president of the Tokyo American Club. Mr. Collins has published three works of fiction on the general theme of U.S.-Japan relations and writes a weekly column in *The Japan Times*.

Mr. Collins and his wife, Keiko—whom he met in college more years ago than either will admit—have one daughter attending a university in the United States (and whose tuition bill is due at any moment).

Mr. Collins lists his hobbies as solving crossword puzzles, worrying about the yen-dollar exchange rate, and mastering the subtleties of a crosscourt backhand drop shot. He speaks fluent Japanese, unless his wife is in the same room.

Japan-Think
. . .
Ameri-Think

An Irreverent Guide to Understanding
the Cultural Differences
Between Us

. . .

ROBERT J. COLLINS

Series Concept by Jane Walmsley

PENGUIN BOOKS

PENGUIN BOOKS
Published by the Penguin Group
Penguin Books USA Inc.,
375 Hudson Street, New York, New York 10014, U.S.A.
Penguin Books Ltd, 27 Wrights Lane,
London W8 5TZ, England
Penguin Books Australia Ltd, Ringwood,
Victoria, Australia
Penguin Books Canada Ltd, 10 Alcorn Avenue,
Toronto, Ontario, Canada M4V 3B2
Penguin Books (N.Z.) Ltd, 182–190 Wairau Road,
Auckland 10, New Zealand

Penguin Books Ltd, Registered Offices:
Harmondsworth, Middlesex, England

First published in Penguin Books 1992

5 7 9 10 8 6 4

LIBRARY OF CONGRESS CATALOGING IN PUBLICATION DATA
Collins, Robert J.
Japan-think, Ameri-think: an irreverent guide to understanding the cultural differences
between us / Robert J. Collins.
p. cm.
ISBN 0 14 01.4860 4
1. Japan—Civilization—1945–   2. United States—Civilization—1970–
3. Comparative civilization.   I. Title.
DS822.5.C65 1992
303.48'273052—dc20   91-18184

Printed in the United States of America
Set in Garamond #3 and Novarese Medium Italic
Designed by Mary A. Wirth

To Keiko and Jen,
the ladies in my life

•   •   •

Contents

· · ·

Japan-Think
. . .
Ameri-Think

Introduction

• • •

It was cloudy that afternoon in 1853 when Commodore Perry's black ships appeared on the horizon. They looked, if anything, like floating temples festooned with holiday banners and streamers.

"Well, I'll be darned," Hiroko said to her husband, Jiro. She had just gotten her two youngest children to bed on the floor for their naps and was preparing to join the other ladies in the village for an afternoon of folding paper replicas of all the creatures of the forest. The Tips of the Rice Plants Are Emerging Above the Water festival was scheduled for the next day—provided, of course, it didn't rain. "Someone must have planned a big surprise for us tomorrow," she added.

Jiro, whose habit it was to use his lunch hour for painting with delicate brush strokes the characters chosen to represent words in his favorite seventeen-syllable poetry, had just rolled up his scrolls and was preparing to join the other men in the village for a session of walking around in water up to their shins to confirm the tip situation.

"I don't know," said Jiro, squinting at the mysterious structures looming even larger as he squinted, "the last surprise we had around here was 709 years ago when the earthquake made Suzuki-san's rice paddy a mountain."

"Then what's going on?" asked Hiroko, her voice betraying a slight panic. The structures were now close enough to observe that they were being driven by hairy monkeys dressed up to look like humans. "Is this somebody's idea of a joke?"

" 'Fraid not," sighed Jiro in resignation. He stored his scrolls in one of the thirty-five drawers of the hand-carved cabinet at his elbow, stood up, and padded in his bare feet over the smooth bamboo tatami to the front door. Other men from the village were already beginning to line up on the shoreline in the time-honored positions of age and rank—the village elders in the center and the others, division heads, department managers, sake brewers, farmers, mailboys, and common serfs, in descending order at the wings—and Jiro had to hurry to take his position between the thirty-two- and thirty-four-year-olds.

"I think what we have here," he said, slipping his flip-flops on and looking down the hill at the shoreline where a most splendidly clad monkey was wading to dry land, "is the end of 250-plus years of noble isolation, the pending doom of Tokugawa's reign, and the possible reestablishment to power of the emperor, probably up in Tokyo. Plus fax machines."

"What?" asked Hiroko.

"And furthermore," continued Jiro, ignoring as always his wife's question, "I have a feeling it's going to be a scramble catching up to whatever these outsiders consider to be, ah, civilization."

• • •

"Whaddya think, Jake?"

Jake was leaning on the ship's railing watching the chaw of tobacco he had just spit over the side bob and weave its way on the gentle waves to where the good Commodore was standing in the shallow water. One had to admit that the Commodore did look impressive with his high boots, buttons of gold, and hat with feathers. He was waving his sword over his head. A regiment of glum peasants, leaning on wooden hoes, formed a row on the shore. They seemed to be conducting desultory conversation among themselves.

"Well," said Jake, looking up at the green mountains in the distance, "I don't think they got anything we'd want." He spit one more time over the side of the ship. "But maybe we can convince them to buy some of our stuff."

Chapter

1

. . .

ESTABLISHING FRAMES

OF REFERENCE

It is indisputable that the following statements require a certain amount of subjective judgment if "understanding" is to be established.

    A. That's a pretty fish.
    B. It sure as hell is crowded around here.
    C. You can count on me.
    D. Oh, you're so big and strong.
    E. It rains a lot.
    F. That's a great idea.
    G. It's just down the road a piece.
    H. The check's in the mail.
    I. I love you, omigod, I love you, I love you.

Creating frames of reference can be tricky business in most situations—even for folks dwelling all their lives next door to each other. The task becomes Herculean when radically different cultures collide. The complete set of gage we carry is both a blessing in the stabil but a burden in the misunderstanding it create different places grow up believing different things. There is nothing profound in that—the key to understanding is instead an awareness of *what* those differences are and, if possible, some glimmer of insight into *why* they exist.

For example, the statement "I do not speak English very well," as uttered by a Japanese, whose language lessons have been torturously long and whose attitudes toward blowing one's own horn are akin to the concept of murdering one's mother on the temple steps, means that the pluperfect tense has not been thoroughly mastered.

On the other hand, the statement "I do speak some Japanese" from an American, whose exposure to the need to speak in foreign tongues is limited to trips to New York and whose very being rebels at the idea of admitting to inadequacies, means that the words "sayonara," "sukiyaki," "sushi," "Honda," "Toyota," and, ah, "sayonara" have been mastered. A neutral observer might note a tendency toward over- and understatement, but in a way, both sides are right.

Or consider a first-time Japanese visitor to America. Invariably there is a great deal of raving about "all the space all over the place." That's understandable; Japan is about the size of California. But what makes the observation about space more remarkable is the fact that the first-time Japanese visitor is not standing on the lip of the Grand Canyon. He is usually in midtown Manhattan during rush hour doing the raving (and wondering where all the people are). To a Japanese, a building across a four-lane street is far away. To an American, the building would have to be hovering near the horizon to qualify.

"Crowding" is an issue unto itself. A horrendous traffic jam in and around the expressways and tunnel to the airport in Boston does not even begin to stack up to mere "slow-downs" on Tokyo's roads on lazy afternoons. Nightmares on the Ventura Freeway during morning rush hours duplicate conditions in Tokyo—literally and at the same time. While Californians crawl along, Japanese are doing the same thing. But in Tokyo, it's after midnight.

First-time American visitors to Japan invariably rave about "how polite and considerate everyone seems to be." The Japanese host will make deprecatory noises and gestures as he reflects upon his trip to the office that day—a trip involving among other things nearly being run over by a kid on a motorcycle, physically fighting his way onto a commuter train, being kicked in the knee by a lady he beat to the last available seat, losing his shoe on the subway platform when a high school girl stepped on his heel, having an umbrella tip jammed into his ear, and suffering the indignity of being lectured by his boss all the way from the entrance to the office building up to his work station with constructive criticism implying that a transfer to Borneo was in the cards if he didn't "put more time into the job." And here was his American guest rhapsodizing about a normal cup of green tea and a hot towel.

"Japanese and Westerners may appear to be doing the same thing," observed Lafcadio Hearn around the turn of the century, "but they're doing them for different reasons." Lafcadio got it right, as far as he went. Japanese and Westerners also do *opposite* things for the *same* reasons. A study of nature's laws of *Time, Space,* and *Motion* within cultural contexts may help.

· Time ·

AMERI-TIME is money. It's as simple as that. Someone earning $50,000 a year is really earning 43.4 cents a working minute. ("Miss Smith, get me the Coast. And for godsakes hurry!") It takes Dwight Gooden slightly under six seconds to wind up and deliver a pitch. That is, for him, $2.15 worth of labor. A recent hero in the American junk bond arena, currently cooling his heels in a federal slammer, once boasted that he made $48 million in the time it took to make two phone calls. History does not record if the phone was push button or dial, but a conservative estimate indicates income amassing at the rate of $12 million a minute.

American corporate culture operates within a time frame perfectly suited for the needs of the moment. Short-term profits should be realized before noon on Friday. All cash in the pipeline should be blown through by the end of the month. Quarterly figures had better reflect positive response to the long-range planning scheme or there'll be hell to pay. Two depressed quarters in a row could start heads rolling. A bad year is obscene, and heralds the arrival of specialists in the arcane science of mergers, acquisitions, and divestitures. Buzzards circle at the fifteenth month.

JAPAN-TIME is what happens between now and then. Europeans refined the measurement of time from the hour-glasses of the Middle East to the mechanical wheels, weights, and balances of the Renaissance. The French painted pretty pictures on enameled dials, Germans concocted elaborate counterweighted machines employing stones from the fields, and the Swiss for some reason thought cuckoos would add luster to the measurement process. America, composed of people from all those places, made further refinements in the form of watch casings capable of withstanding falls from great heights onto sharp rocks and lengthy interment in sharks' bowels.

But it is Japan that revolutionized the manufacturing process. The world's largest seller of timepieces has devised a way to construct measurement instruments with only three or four moving parts—employing robots. Notwithstanding England's Greenwich demarcation, Japan controls the world's "time" market.

Yet time is measured in Japanese offices by calendars. Clocks are rarely nailed to the wall. In fact, two-month calendars are preferred. Remember, it was never really clear when the tips of the rice plants would in fact emerge above the water—the only certainty was that the mandatory festival should end before the Draining the Fields ceremonies began.

Japanese corporations take a "long view" of things that is off the chart of any comparable American corporation. "Relationships" are deemed to be more important. ("They supplied silkworms to us, we built their warehouses, they funded our bank, we hired their founder's great-grandson, they owe us for the 1946 loan, and our Ministry of Finance liaison officer is descended from a rice farmer named Jiro who was related by marriage to their president's ancestors.") Without the pressures from stockholders, who as individuals are lucky to have a small piece of the action, "urgency" is not a word one uses in describing behavior within the group. Try getting a decision by Thursday in Japan ("We'll look into it right away"), and one comes to appreciate a whole new definition of "time." And it has nothing to do with what Seiko's doing.

· Space ·

AMERI-SPACE is something to be filled. "Go West, young man, go West." Horace Greeley's advice, despite the fact that he was referring to Michigan at the time, signaled a pioneering spirit that has affected generations of Americans. The Conestoga Wagon Company, advertising in handbills distributed in Brooklyn, touted the wonders of traveling through the newly tamed territories beyond the Mississippi. "The sky's the limit," echoed the railroaders and their investors, and soon the wagon trails were paralleled by iron horse right-of-ways. Frederic Remington filled his canvases with cowboys, horses, campfires, sagebrush, cacti, tumbleweeds, and blue-gray mountains—all in one eight-by-ten painting. Americans and nature were at one in both abhorring a vacuum.

JAPAN-SPACE is something to be preserved, if at all possible created, and in any event treasured. Classic Japanese paintings might be composed of a few scrawny tree branches breaking into the scene from the right, a two-stroke rendering of Mt. Fuji in the background, and a wavy line representing a distant bird. What turns people on is not the brushwork—it's the empty stuff in between.

On May 30, 1990, the population of Japan hit the magic number of 123,456,789. Although the country is physically the size of California, precipitous mountains and live volcanoes limit the habitable territory to about 30 percent of the whole (which, incidentally, the civilians must share with the farmers). Imagine, for one horrifying moment, the equivalent of half the population of America living cheek by jowl in an area not much larger than the flat parts of southern California. ("Space? Oh, yeah, I remember that.")

· Motion ·

AMERI-MOTION is taken for granted. It's relatively easy to "get there." Commuting to and from the workplace, making the ten o'clock appointment at the dentist, and strolling to the restaurant for a lunch date all lend themselves to a simple "time-space" analysis. Of course, there is the occasional accident on the Outer Drive, a hang-up at the left-turn signal in front of the drugstore, and the eight-ten from Bronxville might lose power, a wheel, or its way, but in the ordinary course of the day these are exceptions rather than the rule.

Young Executive Women can do the calculations, put on their sneakers, and walk all the way from midtown Manhattan to Wall Street in time for work with only stop-lights and open manholes impeding their progress.

JAPAN-MOTION is everything. Since there is no "space" (in the sense of open, definable emptiness between things), and "time" is relative to calendars, "motion" must be concentrated upon. In those circumstances it becomes dangerous to stand still—one could be mistaken for a tree and chopped down (to make more space) or suffer the indignity of having letters posted in the mouth. Inanimate, in Japan, means dead.

As for the Japanese commuting adventure, distances have no real meaning in the Western sense. It's difficult seeing the horizon when there's so much in between. If one happens to live where the meandering bus to the train station stops, if the train itself happens to go somewhere near a relevant subway system, if the subway exits in a spot where the police happen to be allowing taxis to line up, the two-and-a-half-hour trip can be a piece of cake. (A crow, making the same commute, might note that the overall distance is not much greater than that between the two tips of Manhattan island.) If the unlucky commuter happens *not* to live near any of the aforementioned connection points, the trip could take even longer although the crow overhead only flies half as far.

"Why not walk?" ask the commuters in sneakers. Well, it's not that simple. Picture a square with you standing at one corner. Your target destination is a dot in the center of the square. The shortest distance between two points is a straight line, right? The problem is that in Japan there are no straight lines. The happy commuter must contrive to reach several of the other corners of the square before accessing a route that more or less wanders in the dot's direction. And this does not take into account the very real danger of getting lost. It is understood and accepted in Japan that people in one square have absolutely no concept of where they are relative to neighboring squares.

So "motion" in Japan is where it's at. While the American from Webster Grove proceeds in stately fashion from home to office—usually arriving on time—his Japanese counterpart runs to catch Bus No. 12, dashes up and down stairs and around corners in train stations, races to join several tens of thousands of his compatriots in the subway, chases a taxi down the middle of the street, scurries through the basements of buildings and past construction sites, leaps into elevators just as the doors close, and gets to the office, depending on his luck along the way, either an hour early or an hour late.

To appreciate the significance of it all, examine the statement "Drop in with your family sometime this weekend" in light of the two cultural reference frames as applied to time, space, and motion. "Dropping in" will probably not occur in either country—but for different reasons. The Americans probably don't mean it, and no one's disappointed. The Japanese probably *do* mean it, but there are situations in life when "you can't get there from here" is really true.

2

· · ·

LOVE, SEX, AND MARRIAGE
(SEX, MARRIAGE, AND LOVE)

· Meeting the Opposite Sex ·

IN AMERI-THINK, "the luck of the draw" principle applies as much as anything else. In a country made great by wild-catters and poker players, "it ain't such a bad system." The fact notwithstanding that approximately one out of two marriages winds up on the trash heap, the ideal of democratic opportunity still applies. Geographic proximity affects the selection process—the boy or girl next door, the school class-mate, the person in the front row of the church choir, or the piece of work on the next barstool tend to have the odds in their favor. In fact, about the only outside influence on the selection process is usually a negative one. "If you bring him around here one more time, I'm gonna shoot him. He has another girl's name tattooed on his forehead." Or, "I've met a lot of girls in my time, son, and we had names for people like her." Curiously, *positive* suggestions about prospective candidates are made at everyone's risk. There is the very real danger that the suggestions will condemn the candidate to permanent dorkhood.

JAPAN-THINK allows a certain amount of random access—in fact it's virtually impossible to avoid random access unless one is a Buddhist monk up in the mountains—but anything more serious than a group date involving several dozen couples is frowned upon without prior clearance and a whole lot of background checking. Obviously there are exceptions to this, but in general the economic, societal, and familial partnership represented by marriage is too basic to things to allow a couple of damn fool kids to make the decision on their own. "Dating," as a social exercise, is fine and dandy, but don't jump to conclusions about it having anything to do with potential marriage partnerships.

· Getting Serious ·

AMERI-THINK realizes that talk of "love" is an indication that the relationship has gone from the mundane to the serious. "Being in love" is an inalienable right guaranteed by the Constitution of the United States of America (or if it's not, it should be, by God). Young boys and girls are seldom able to escape their grade-school years without being "partnered" for one social occasion or another. AMERI-THINK supports the Romeo and Juliet principle, and cultural heroes are often those who, against all odds and without any support, prevailed in their love, rode out the storm of opposition, and drove the Chevrolet off to a lifetime of marital bliss. Incidentally, it is at the "love" stage, if one is to believe the surveys, that the relationship more often than not is confirmed by sex, irrespective of the marriage date.

Meanwhile, JAPAN-THINK dictates that after six or seven years of harmlessly fooling around in random-access group dates, it's time to get married. At twenty-eight, the average age of marriage for men, and twenty-five, the average age of marriage for women, one must get serious. The men will have received at least five annual raises from their employers, two-room apartments can be afforded, and further delays in the matrimonial pilgrimage might cause the whispers to start about an "inability to fit into society."

Women in Japan approach the magic age of marriage with considerable trepidation. If age twenty-five comes and goes without any prospects, she moves from the category of "Office Lady Working Just Until Marriage" to the onerous "Office Lady Working Quite Possibly Forever." Each month beyond the magic age decreases her prospects since the three-year spread between husbands and wives is deemed most desirable, and the only men left for her at that stage are the ones who indeed have an "inability to fit into society."

While AMERI-THINK allows people to walk into crowded rooms blindfolded, JAPAN-THINK looks very pragmatically at the prospective household. Friends, relatives, and especially business connections are employed to "introduce" suitable candidates to each other. (An adjunct to the search process in this electronic age is the relatively new industry of computerized matchmaking. Dozens of firms pop up each month, and it is estimated that in 1989 over one million Japanese took advantage of the services to meet prospective mates.)

Relative positions of the families are considered, educational background is explored, hobbies are examined, and in the prospective husband's case the "name" of his employers is bandied about. It is a whole lot better, in the grand scheme of things, to be working for a Mitsubishi company than Watanabe Plumbing Supplies. To be asked by a family to be a "go-between" in the marriage brokering rigmarole is to be highly honored, but it carries a responsibility that extends to being available to help solve any disputes that might occur years after the marriage has been consummated.

As a point of interest, over one thousand detective agencies exist in Japan for the sole purpose of confirming (or digging up) background information about prospective marriage partners. On the surface, Japan is a homogeneous country, but there are categories within categories. The descendants of aborigines (Ainu), Koreans (at least within the last ten or eleven generations), and outcasts (who had the misfortune to be assigned to jobs no one else would do three hundred years ago) put a different slant on things. Young Japanese tend to be less concerned about all this, but there's always Great Aunt Koko to think about. And since she's a member of the family, she's thought about.

It is sometime during the "getting serious" stage that sex enters the picture, but unlike AMERI-THINK, JAPAN-THINK does not yet recognize the existence of love. After a series of "introduced" dates—during which the girl demurely examines over and over again her plate in the restaurant while the boy quizzes her carefully about her hobbies—is when we move to the intimate plateau. After all, reports from investigators and family friends are beginning to trickle in, and no genealogical surprises appear to be buried in the lacquerwork. "Compatibility" can now be tested.

AMERI-THINK considers premarital sex to be something to accomplish whenever the opportunity arises. The couple is in love, and passion begets creativity. Exhaustive research reveals the following venues as being acceptable in the circumstances:

A. The back seat of the family sedan
B. The front seat of the family sedan
C. The couch of those nice people down the street who pay five dollars per hour for baby-sitting

D. On top of the photocopy machine in the mailroom
E. In the choir loft
F. Under a blanket at the beach
G. On the blanket at the beach (nights only)
H. In the park where nobody goes
I. At the library in the antiquities room
J. In the front *and* back seat of the family sedan

JAPAN-THINK will not permit any of the above. First of all, the family sedan is cripplingly small (and there's no place to park it except the family living room), mothers won't allow baby-sitters within ten kilometers of their children (more about this later), the photocopy machine is in the lobby of the building's main entrance (remember the space limitations in Japan), beaches are shoulder-to-shoulder with people (or fishermen) day and night, and the antiquities room at the library is full of scholars studying the seventeen-syllable poetry written by people like Jiro (before the foreign devils arrived). Choir lofts don't exist.

There is a more fundamental reason for JAPAN-THINK not permitting the above. Compatibility is being tested, and tests should be conducted under the best of all possible conditions. Into this void in the market surges the "love hotel" phenomenon.

Love hotels charge by the hour. The minimum charge is two hours—the maximum is open-ended. However, love hotel managers routinely check the facilities every twenty-four hours to make certain no one has died on the premises. Structures of fantasy that make Disney's Magic Kingdom look prosaic by comparison, there are more of them in Japan than gas stations.

Make no mistake, they are not houses of prostitution. This was reaffirmed recently by two visiting businessmen from overseas who checked in, and after calling down to the front desk for beers every fifteen minutes or so (and subtly letting it be known "they were available"), the light dawned. (They then contrived to slink out with the humbling awareness that the manager thought the facilities were for *them*.)

One must bring one's own partner to a love hotel. So for the purposes of checking compatibility, JAPAN-THINK encourages the use of the love hotel.

There are rooms that duplicate the Palace at Versailles, a Wild West saloon, Roman spas, torture chambers of Henry VIII's era, Tahitian verandas, Martian landscapes, and Italian bordellos. Remember, the testers of compatibility are not "in love," and all contributions to the atmosphere of romance are gratefully accepted. As of this writing (note to the publishers: research on this has been awesome and expense vouchers are being sent under separate cover), the very most popular rooms feature dry-ice-produced clouds of vapor which shoot out at bed level. This produces the effect of copulating, one presumes, in heaven. The family sedan just does not measure up.

AMERI-THINK refers to an orgasm as "coming."

JAPAN-THINK considers it to be "going."

· The Ceremony ·

AMERI-THINK believes that the wedding ceremony should resemble a three-ring circus staged primarily for the family and relatives of the bride and groom. (The bride herself is permitted some "input," usually in the form of guest-list approval.) Few Americans are involved in any other event in their lives where social protocol is so significant. Advice and etiquette columnists build entire careers answering questions in the following categories:

A. *Gifts* ("If I don't like the patterns selected by the bride, can't I give her my favorite fork?")

B. *Relatives* ("My daughter wants to invite her aunt to the reception, but she knows damn well that my sister is a slut and we don't speak.")

C. *Exes* ("Just because her father's paying for it, does the son of a bitch have a right to show up?")

D. *Grandparents* ("We live on a fixed income of $168.50 a month, 6,352 miles away. Can we just send a card instead?")

E. *New in-laws* ("His Uncle Buck drinks too much. Can we put up signs in the bar saying 'Don't Serve Buck'?")

F. *Bridesmaids, grooms, et al.* ("The dresses the other girls chose don't match my eyes, plus the best man's parole officer won't let him . . .)

The end result, despite all the preparatory concerns, is that the American wedding is a rather balanced mixture of dignity, romantic touches, some pathos, and good social fun (particularly if Uncle Buck gets to the hard stuff).

• • •

In JAPAN-THINK, protocol is already established. The rules are clear, have been for years, and no one questions them. In fact, the only questions related to the wedding ceremony are:

A. "Where is it?"
B. "How the hell do I get there?"

Keep in mind, the guest list and seating arrangements are determined by the same traditions dictating the positions of the villagers the day Commodore Perry's ship came to town. The village elders—"elder" not only in raw age but in "importance" (i.e., job) in the community—get the good seats up front. This means the groom's boss comes first, followed by his favorite teacher, who in turn are followed by the bride's boss and her favorite teacher. Various working colleagues are next, and then relatives and old school pals (seated in the corners). Way in the back of the room, included almost as an afterthought and assuming there's enough space, are the parents of the bride and groom. The "go-between" and his or her spouse get to sit at the head table with the lucky young couple.

After the Shinto priest goes through the ritual—no one is very clear in Japan what the ritual means (and the priests are wisely closed-lipped on the subject)—a reception is stage-managed by special individuals hired by the hotel or wedding hall for the purpose. (No one questions these special individuals either, but they seem to have learned their craft by watching old Doris Day movies and reading "*Life* Goes to a Party.")

JAPAN-THINK considers all formal occasions to be incomplete without a series of long, rambling speeches, beginning with representatives of the village elders and continuing at sporadic intervals all the way down to the serfs. During these times, the bride and groom change costumes repeatedly. It all starts with the traditional wedding kimono and wigs, then proceeds to "Western" white gown and tails, devolves to a modern cocktail dress and a slightly less formal but often pastel tuxedo, and winds up with "traveling clothes" direct from the pages of *Country Gentleman*.

JAPAN-THINK permits no, repeat no, mingling of guests between tables. Uncle Buckita could become seriously plastered, but the only people who'd know would be the other seven at his table. One moment of true emotion occurs at the very end of the party when, as the guests are itching to leave and the newlyweds are worrying about the departure time of the Japan Airlines jet to Hawaii, the fathers of the bride and groom make brief statements about how happy they are that "all matters are settled."

AMERI-THINK dictates that the bride and groom be showered with gifts galore—some of which, like Aunt Isabel's silver candlestick holders, cannot be effectively employed until somewhere around the tenth wedding anniversary.

JAPAN-THINK insists upon pragmatism. The wedding guests, in discreet little envelopes made for the purpose, contribute cash. The amount, depending upon one's rank on the shoreline, ranges from $150 to $1,000—all for the honor of being included in the festivities.

Incidentally, JAPAN-THINK now allows thoughts of love to creep up within the married couple, and it usually happens within three or four years.

Chapter

3

. . .

SETTLING IN AT HOME

· Finding a Place ·

It is not easy being a newlywed. That's universal. It would be a whole lot easier if economic circumstances could be reversed—magnificent housing for the young who are still experimenting with each other, and modest quarters for the experienced who have learned how to stay out of each other's way.

AMERI-THINK knows that the natural progression of things calls for increasingly larger homesteads until the time, when the kids have gone and retirement settles in, that modest contractions in space are necessary so as to fit into a condo at Fort Lauderdale or a villa in Sun City. Along the way apartments with hot and cold running water (in buildings with elevators), cozy little cottages (behind white picket fences), suburban estates (on acres of land), and convenient town houses (minutes from the office) are realizable dreams.

JAPAN-THINK knows only one thing about housing—
it will be a scramble finding *anything* at *anytime* even remotely
providing enough space. Newlyweds will consider themselves
extremely fortunate if a spare room in either set of parents'
homes is available for the posthoneymoon breaking-in period.
Private space measuring nine feet by twelve feet would be
ideal—especially considering that the kitchen would only
have to be shared by one other wife.

Major corporations do provide dormitory housing for
single employees (with common dining, bath, and toilet facilities), and one-room self-contained units for married employees. Family planning follows the husband's career
course—older and higher ranking employees qualify for two-
and sometimes three-room units.

An American political leader, upon returning from his
first trip to Japan, remarked to the press that the Japanese
"all live in rabbit hutches." That upset many Japanese. They
know rabbit hutches are often larger.

· Paying for It ·

AMERI-THINK understands the generally accepted standard
of pegging mortgage or rent payments at a level somewhere
around one-third disposable income. The standard is not always followed—family circumstances or a particularly attractive "dream house" can nudge the percentage to something
approaching half of disposable income. Generally speaking,
the investment is sound and the living conditions are comfortable. Why not go for it? It's the American Dream.

JAPAN-THINK knows that housing even approaching
the space afforded by the average American bungalow would
run to four or five times disposable income. It is at this point
that a very basic decision is made. "Going for it," in JAPAN-
THINK, has nothing to do with housing.

· *Disposable Income* ·

JAPAN	AMERICA
1. Entertainment	1. Housing
2. Education	2. Education
3. Housing	3. Entertainment

JAPAN-THINK allows a compromise when it comes to housing. "The cottage with the white picket fence around it is way beyond the reasonable expectations of all but lunatics; let's have fun in other ways." Japanese housing becomes, therefore, some place to cool heels in between adventures out in public.

For example, consider the uses put to housing in Japan and America.

JAPAN	AMERICA
A. Sleeping	A. Slumber parties, king-size beds, separate vanities, walk-in closets, orgies
B. Eating	B. Dining, guests, parties, buffet tables, eat-in kitchens, breakfast nooks
C.	C. Dens, studies, second offices, work stations, sewing rooms, nurseries, playrooms
D.	D. Castle security, sanctity in isolation, a retreat, hedge against inflation

In a way, JAPAN-THINK envies the available space in America, but in another way it considers itself to be fortunate in *not* being tied down to a heavy mortgage, serious maintenance concerns, and the problems of little disposable cash at the end of the month.

AMERI-THINK accepts assets in housing.

JAPAN-THINK prefers cash in the bank.

Chapter

4

. . .

ENTERTAINMENT
AND LEISURE TIME

"Entertainment" as a word covers a lot of territory—as well it should. In general, it means everything one does to amuse, thrill, relax, intrigue, broaden, excite, and exhaust oneself. It means going somewhere to see or do something as well as acquiring things to have these things done for you. Going out to watch the Super Bowl or purchasing a new television set to see it at home all involve expenses lumpable in the category of "entertainment."

"Leisure time," on the other hand, is relatively easy to define. It means those periods in the day, week, month, or year when all the things one is supposed to do are done.

AMERI-THINK, as a rule, considers "entertainment" to be a function of "leisure time"—"when we have time, we'll have fun." Once the grass is mowed, the screens put up, the dishes done, the kids driven home, the hallway painted, and the garage cleaned, we'll go to the movies. Adult league softball games are never scheduled on Thursday mornings during the work week. Dramas at the local playhouse are not performed on Monday afternoons. Only things like watching television, listening to music, or practicing juggling in the living room can be squeezed in without a large block of "leisure time" set aside for the purpose.

JAPAN-THINK views the whole business a little differently. First of all, for the average working man or woman, arriving home at 11:00 P.M. after a two-hour commute, then preparing oneself to turn around and leave at 6:30 A.M. for the trek back to the grind, "leisure time" becomes only those hours on Sunday morning when it is possible to do the one thing 87 percent of working Japanese reported in a recent poll they would rather do than anything else—sleep. Christianity will never take hold in Japan in a big way. When else but Sunday mornings can people sleep? Not only that, once Sunday noon rolls around, the salaryman with a family *must* take the kids out from under foot and perform his once-a-week "parental duty" by taking them off to a park or amusement area. There's nothing "leisure" about that. Public areas in Japan on Sunday afternoons are full of men walking around with little kids and wishing they were back in their offices.

JAPAN-THINK considers "leisure time" to be:

A. The period of time between birth and kindergarten
B. The period of time between final retirement and death
C. The period of time when, because the office is closed anyway, he must—gun held to his head—take a four-day vacation

Despite the above, more disposable income in Japan is spent on "entertainment" than anything else. How can that be, you ask? It's simple. In Japan "entertainment" is not a function of "leisure time." It is instead part of the fabric of life—a "life-style" if you will.

It is commonly known that the Japanese are, to put it mildly, golf fanatics. There are times when three of the seven major television networks will run golf programs at the same time in prime time. A rainy-day danger is not the possibility of being poked in the eye by an umbrella—it is the real potential of being whapped over the head by salarymen practicing their golf swings on subway platforms with their umbrellas. Eight out of ten Japanese corporate salarymen have spent time practicing golf, even if it's nothing more than repetitious sessions at the driving range. But is that time "leisure time"? Not really. It's part of the job. Golf courses are busier on weekdays during business hours than they are on weekends.

Or take the simple function of eating. AMERI-THINK considers, other than lunchtime meals, that going out to eat four or five times a month is adequately civilized, and something that falls into the entertainment/leisure time category. JAPAN-THINK knows that going out to eat four or five times *a week* could lead to serious malnutrition problems. What is happening the other two or three days per week? When the workaday world involves late hours in the office and long sessions of romancing business contacts and associates—and home is two or three hours away—how better to spend the time than in an agreeable and impressive restaurant?

And where does one draw the line between "business" and "personal" time? When corporations provide their employees with facilities for sporting, cultural, educational, and entertainment clubs and associations, going out and paying for goods and services to supplement the sponsored activities becomes, well, part of life. A night on the town with the gang from the office, after a rigorous session of flower-arranging practice, is as common as crab grass in suburbia. (JAPAN-THINK permits company-sponsored athletic teams to play games whenever ballfields are available—even if it's Thursday morning during the work week.)

· Spouse Involvement ·

AMERI-THINK is, if nothing else, democratic. Since "entertainment" is usually relegated to leisure time, and since the availability (or extent) of cash remaining after housing and necessity expenditures is a factor, the precious resources must be allocated carefully. Everyone in the family, to varying degrees, has a vote, and "entertainment" becomes a group endeavor. Whether it's a decision to purchase a Land Rover, to agree upon a camping ground for vacaction, to go to the opera on Saturday, or to acquire a video recorder to tape high school football games, the spouse is involved. Entertainment and leisure time are together compartmentalized in AMERI-THINK, and the family unit is the beneficiary.

JAPAN-THINK permits democracy up to a point. But since "entertainment" opportunities and possibilities exist at varying times throughout the day or night, and since most waking hours are somehow related to work, job, or profession, spouses are not even in the same ballpark—at least Monday through Friday. This certainly applies when one spouse is home with the children, but it also applies with two working spouses. The operative unit, except for those Sunday afternoons in the park, is primarily the employee group.

AMERI-THINK has introduced a baffling and worrisome custom to Japan through the joint-venture and branch office systems established in Tokyo and Osaka. In an attempt to demonstrate their "internationalism," Japanese executives go along with it, but with wind-sucking reluctance. Cocktail parties, with the wives of visiting businessmen in attendance, are held after work in center-city hotels or in the spacious (by Japanese standards) apartments of expatriate American executives. Japanese executives and coworkers are invited to these parties—mundane as they are by American standards—and they are expected to be there with their wives.

Ah, the agony of it all. To convince a wife living two hours away to drop dinner preparations for the children, put on a dress "that Westerners will like," jump on the bus, train, and subway, find a cab driver during rush hour, get to the hotel or apartment, and then stand around looking sophisticated while everyone else is babbling in a foreign tongue is to tax the most solidly arranged marriage. Worse yet, a great deal of time must be spent by the wife during the evening "pretending" to be the husband's equal (more on this later) when in fact most of her life is spent "pretending" to be her husband's servitor. This can even be difficult for the husband. ("Vacation? I am not . . . ah, *we* haven't, er, discussed our plans yet.")

Considering the options open to the Japanese businessman, as he puts in the long hours with customers developing relationships, it is small wonder that the spouse is usually nowhere to be found.

JAPAN-THINK *Business Entertainment Category*

1. Drinks with the staff after work. It is accepted in Japan that the rigid hierarchical barriers existing in the workplace must be broached periodically with "open" communication—communication best achieved under the universal leveling effect of alcohol. One may call one's boss a shithead during these sessions, and later plead the defense of drunkenness. It gets things out into the open, releases pressure, and is surprisingly forgotten the next day.

2. Client entertainment. Nothing could be more important—and corporate Japan expects to pay for it. Depending upon relationships, dinner after work in an exclusive restaurant and a full Las Vegas—type show afterwards can run to several thousand dollars—easily. A business relationship that has mellowed, that can withstand more personal interaction than that possible in formal settings, may go down the scale a bit in cost, but up the scale in hedonistic activities. Sitting together in shirtsleeves eating chicken parts grilled on a stick, drinking beer, going off to watch a strip-tease show and drinking watered whiskey, then concluding the night bellowing songs into a microphone to the accompaniment of recorded music is very mellowing indeed. And to round it all off with a bowl of noodles and more beer before the last train home will cement relationships for at least a month.

3. Hostess bars. These establishments provide a venue for more relaxed conversation, coupled with sexual titillation, before, during, or after any of the above-mentioned activities. From a variety of backgrounds, hostesses may be aging refugees from the more rigid geisha profession, girls from next door, secretaries supplementing their income, or college kids piling up money for trips abroad. Sprinkled among them are "entertainers" from Southeast Asia and "models" from the Western world. The ambience is "hotel living room," with shin-bruising tiny tables and low-slung stuffed chairs and couches. The point of it all is to sit around and "discuss business" while attractive and attentive young lovelies vie for the honor of lighting your cigarettes, pouring your drinks, and rubbing your thigh. The result of it all is an elevated ego and libido, but precious little else. Actual sexual activity is rare—most trains stop running at midnight.

Compared to the above, AMERI-THINK's business entertainment category pales by comparison.

1. 7:30 A.M. "power breakfast" at the Hyatt
2. A two-hour lunch with a glass of white wine followed by oceans of Perrier
3. Cocktails with the guys from the agency after work but before the six-ten to Stamford

All of this is *not* to say that Japanese husbands and wives live totally separate lives. Japan has nineteen national holidays (compared to eleven in America and ten in Arizona) and these, coupled with some creative calendar juggling, can be transformed by ignoring random Mondays and Fridays into close to a month of "time off" in sporadic bits and pieces. Families, particularly the young couples without children, do go out and spend time together. Activities of choice are as follows:

1. Trips to Disneyland outside Tokyo. Mickey Mouse decals and Minnie Mouse dolls (stuffed) are the souvenirs of choice.
2. Any of the two-dozen "sea worlds"—featuring whales, performing dolphins, and cute little seals. The seals (stuffed) are the souvenirs of choice.
3. Trips to hot-spring bathing areas. A decal indicating the resort's name and pandas (stuffed) are the souvenirs of choice.
4. Going skiing—but only during "ski season" (December 28 to March 15). It makes no difference what the condition of snow is. One doesn't go early, or late. Little wooden replicas of Bavarian houses and "ski bunnies" (stuffed) are the souvenirs of choice.
5. When the budget is tight, an increasing alternative is converting yen to dollars and traveling to Waikiki in Hawaii. Louis Vuitton purses, Chanel perfume, Johnnie Walker Black, Cartier watches, Ralph Lauren

shirts, and Sampler chocolates (stuffed) are the souvenirs of choice.

As a point of interest, JAPAN-THINK considers it mandatory to festoon the family car with the souvenirs from these
trips until it becomes difficult to see out the windows. Then
the souvenirs must be brought to the office for display in and
around desks, the photocopy machine (in the lobby), and the
tea-making room.

Chapter

5

. . .

TRAVEL

Travel, going from one place to another, is for some one of life's great pleasures. It is for others an experience best avoided—like root canal work.

America was settled by travelers. (Even the American Indians came from somewhere, probably Japan.) Originally, great oceans were crossed, broad plains were traversed, and tall mountains were conquered. "Getting there," wherever that was, became the burning ambition of millions. The object was the important thing, not the process.

Even in today's America, going from one place to another is an activity wherein the goal is more often paramount, not the trip itself. Getting to Miami Beach before it's time to turn around and go back, going up from Dallas to visit grandma and grandpa in Chicago at Christmas, whipping across the entire state of Pennsylvania to make graduation ceremonies in Philadelphia, trekking to Seattle to make a brother's wedding, going from Big Ten country to see a Rose Bowl game in southern California. When vacation time rolls around, there's a lot to be said for just going up to the cottage at the lake and cooling it for a while.

Japan, meanwhile, has had a relatively stable population for centuries—no one *had* to go from somewhere to somewhere else, at least in genetic memory. And because it's a small country geographically, "seeing something new" means leaving the islands and going abroad.

It is very important to keep one thing in mind, however. It really *is* cheaper for Japanese with the strong yen to convert to dollars and travel to Hawaii and Guam than it is to go to a first-class resort hotel and spa in Japan by air or rail. That boggles many minds, including Japanese minds.

With the exception of land prices (which for supply and demand reasons are way beyond anything comparable on this planet), the costs of goods and services in Japan are not essentially different, relative to income, than the same costs in other technologically advanced nations. A good dinner and a night in a hotel, a new stereo sound system, or tuition in a private school will cost a Japanese family the same proportion of gross income as it would an American family. The same applies to a cup of coffee. What makes the difference is the conversion in currency. The cup of coffee, converted to American dollars, can be as much as $7. One is better off— is one not?—going abroad with that $7 and buying a steak dinner. And remember, without the burden of mortgage payments, the potential Japanese traveler has a greater proportion of his income dedicated to "entertainment and leisure time."

JAPAN-THINK believes *everyone* should travel abroad— at least once, for the good of the soul and for the purpose of becoming "international." This belief is strongly supported by all who know things about "abroad"—Japan Airlines, the Japan Travel Bureau, major Japanese hotel chains, the Duty-

Free Shoppers folks, and several department store chains. The fact that these organizations have contrived to keep Japanese money within the loop by providing all facilities in many of the destinations abroad is lost on all but the most sophisticated traveler. Similar "motivation" is nonexistent in America.

AMERI-THINK *Preferred International Travel Destinations*

1. Nowhere (unless a student and backpacking or retired and bored with Boca Raton)
2. England (They speak a form of English over there.)
3. Germany (Grandpa Fritz still has a sister alive.)
4. The islands (somewhere, anywhere, in the Caribbean if east of the Mississippi, Hawaii otherwise)
5. New Mexico (Blankets can be purchased with U.S. dollars.)

JAPAN-THINK *Preferred International Travel Destinations*

1. Guam and Hawaii (The loop is as complete as complete can be, and with luck the traveler won't have to deal with locals in any form or fashion.)
2. California (meaning the Universal Studio tour, Disneyland yet again, the boardwalk at Santa Monica, shopping on Rodeo Drive in Beverly Hills, and photographing the HOLLYWOOD sign. Trolley cars and the Golden Gate Bridge are not quite "California" and that's a separate trip anyway.)
3. New York (There is a special thrill, like picking a scab to see what's going on underneath, in walking around for five days in a state of terror.)
4. The United States (Different than the aforementioned locations, much of it is a vague blur, although it's ru-

mored there's another Disney thing in a place called Florida.)

5. Europe (all those places, as quickly as possible and in a big group. Excepting England, where they speak a form of English, the natives are more incoherent than usual. Not only that, the loop is in its infancy.)

6. Hong Kong (It's cheap while it lasts.)

7. Southeast Asia (You can get laid for the price of a cup of coffee and be photographed against interesting backgrounds.)

An interesting phenomenon is developing, however. Experienced as they are in going abroad, albeit originally in large groups, many Japanese travelers are making return trips. And they are doing it on their own! A young Japanese couple was recently overheard to say, apropos of a miniherd of American dentists and their families visiting Honolulu, "They seem to do everything in groups."

Chapter

6

. . .

CONDUCTING BUSINESS

Probably no subject has commanded more media attention in recent years than the topic of Japanese business practices. Scholarly works, bolstered by charts, graphs, and statistics, compete for space on bookshelves with primers on how to bow, exchange business cards, and back out of a room smiling.

If one had a nickel for every televised debate in which the phrases "level playing field," "restraint of trade," "open (or closed) markets," "free access," and the acronym "GATT" appeared, one could go a long way toward solving the balance-of-trade problems with just those nickels.

Theories on the issue include, from AMERI-THINK:
A. Japan is not playing fair.
B. America has been inept in penetrating the Japanese market to the same extent as Japan has penetrated ours.

C. Gratitude for past financial help should be recipro-
cated by Japan adopting voluntary export controls.
D. The Japanese management style is superior.
E. America is too naïve in trying to play fair.
F. Japan is the most important trading partner America
has.
G. Japan, unable to conquer the world militarily, is now
trying to do it economically.

JAPAN-THINK theories include:
A. America should get its own house in order before it
criticizes others.
B. Having no natural resources, we have to export to pay
for imports.
C. We have special, special interests, and they must be
protected.
D. Our markets are really open, you just don't understand our distribution system.
E. If America manufactured products to our standards
we would accept more of them.
F. America is the most important trading partner Japan
has.
G. We are practicing the trade principles we learned from
you.

What is interesting, and perhaps a bit daunting, is that all
or at least parts of all of the above are true. Each country has
its own interests (there is nothing remarkable about that) and
each country goes about protecting its own interests within
the social framework and cultural structure of that country.
Would a muffler repairman from Akron, Ohio, expect bar-
gaining on *his* terms with an Arab sheik with a faulty exhaust
system? Not if he's wise. And by the same token, would a

Dutch florist automatically agree to all terms presented by a New Orleans businessman? Only if he's been in the flower game for a couple of weeks. Compromise, give-and-take, and, dare it be said, exploiting needs and weaknesses is the stuff of successful commerce. Mr. Hunter, with the fur of the jump-prancer-who-runs-in-the-woods-and-doesn't-mind-the-snow, was successful selling loincloths to Mr. Fisher, who lived-by-the-stream-and-had-permanently-wrinkled-fingers because of a willingness to bargain. One pelt for three trout probably wouldn't do, but four pelts for a trout every time the bright-thing-in-the-night-sky-was-big-and-round could do the trick. (Deals, in those days, were confirmed by martinis— on the rocks.)

The key, of course, is recognizing and appreciating the trading partner's concerns. The point here is not to review statistics and figures—other than to admit the obvious, which is that America is getting clobbered on trade with Japan— but instead to highlight the JAPAN-THINK/AMERI-THINK attitudes and cultural mores that exist in real life. Tactics and strategy are for the next book.

AMERI-THINK considers big business to be good, but not best. The phrase "big business" is used more in a negative connotation than a positive one. ("Big business is the reason we individuals are suffering. They don't give a damn.") Preferable, in many minds, is a parcel of medium-sized businesses all slogging it out in the same marketplace, with the stronger (and most competitive) garnering the bulk of spoils. The sentiments of Charlie Wilson, an early president of General Motors, that "what's good for General Motors is good for America," no longer applies. (The Sherman Anti-Trust Act confirmed that.) Let's face it, "big business" is responsible for pollution, labor exploitation, and unwarranted governmental influence. Or so it's said. Big business is considered "good" when the giants (IBM, Kodak, NCR, Citibank, Procter & Gamble, Coca-Cola, General Motors, Ford, United Airlines, Caterpillar, *et al.*) line up favorably in international rankings with similar and competing firms. Otherwise, "big business" is something that requires control, for the protection of those less big.

JAPAN-THINK considers big business to be the best, not just good. Why not have Mitsubishi, Mitsui, Sumitomo, Matsushita, Sony, Toyota, and Honda controlling things? It's the only way to compete. The Charlie Wilson philosophy is firmly entrenched in Japan. Big business builds the recreation areas for the citizens, provides cultural facilities (including the purchase of international art masterpieces), and stabilizes society (lifetime employment). More importantly, big business works closely with the government—often hiring officials after they've retired from public service. What could be better?

AMERI-THINK believes in "equal opportunity." All men are born equal, and all men *must* have an equal chance for the golden ring. It's democracy.

JAPAN-THINK believes in not discriminating. There is a subtle but very real difference here. Big is best, but small can compete and win if small is clever, tenacious, and capable enough. Small, however, doesn't get any breaks. Sumo wrestling, Japan's national sport, does not make distinctions by weight or size. Bigger people have a distinct advantage, and generally win most fights. That's as it should be. But a recently retired sumo grand champion, Chiyonofuji, broke most of the all-time records for tournament and career wins. He is small by sumo standards, and is a national hero—confirming by his outstanding performance that one doesn't need breaks or special consideration for success. (As a point of interest, another sport originating in Japan, judo, also did not have weight classifications until the sport became international.

Japan was the last country to accept the classifications.) Fair is fair, and until you knock off the big guy, you're still small.

AMERI-THINK knows the consumer is king. The Ralph Naders of the world, and related busybodies, have seen to that. Their bleatings have struck a responsive chord in the hearts and minds of most American individuals. And why not? Anyone selling a car "unsafe at any speed" deserves the deserts of a righteous and uncompromising public: "We are paying good money for a product; we don't expect to be killed by it." Attorneys specializing in liability law are poised to take the issues to court. How else can the individual be protected from (here we go again) "big business"? (An interesting spectator sport, from the distance of Japan, is watching the American insurance companies annually going through the song and dance of justifying liability insurance rate increases—as if they had anything to do with jury awards.) Somebody has to take responsibility, and who better than a jury of peers to allocate compensation?

JAPAN-THINK considers the consumer to be one step above a serf, but not quite in the category of a freeman. (For crossword puzzle fanatics, the Japanese consumer is an *esne*.) The Japanese consumer, by reason of the prices he is willing to pay to assist the corporate effort, is actually supporting the international expansion of Japanese companies. Canon cameras are cheaper in New York, and not just because of the exchange rate, than they are in Tokyo. Kirin beer, brewed in Japan and exported to California, can be purchased in Los Angeles and imported to Japan cheaper than the cost of the same beer in the neighborhood saketoria. Why is this, and where are the Ralph Naderyamas of Japan?

One must first examine the relationship between "corporate" and "private" Japan. In medieval days, the richer and more successful a lord was, the better it was for the folks surrounding and supplying the castle. That was a pretty good deal—with a certain amount of luck and a good harvest, the lord might expand and take over the estate of the goofy people on the other side of the mountain. Everyone, including the esnes, prospered. In twentieth-century Japan, the situation is even better. Education and diligence can put *anyone* in the lord's castle, and that means someone's watching out for the folks on the outside. There is probably not a family in Japan today that does not have a member—husband, brother, cousin, uncle, sister, nephew, or niece—working for "big business" in Japan. And when that "big business" is doing all the things lords used to do—providing cultural, educational, and recreational facilities—it's difficult getting the general populace whipped up over the price of a camera in New York. It is equally difficult getting someone to stand on his heels and initiate a lawsuit against Toyota because the front wheels of his car fell off. His sister and mother-in-law both honeymooned at Toyota's facilities on the Izu peninsula.

JAPAN-THINK also has a special attitude about liability responsibilities. A famous situation in recent years involved a family that unexpectedly had to leave their suburban home and travel to Tokyo. (Thank goodness it was not a cocktail party with American visitors.) The family left their four-year-old daughter with next-door neighbors. The daughter, playing with the neighbors' children, fell into a stream near the house and drowned. The parents, to everyone's astonishment, sued the neighbors for negligence—and won! The outrage was such that the parents had to give the money back to the neighbors and move out of the community. The general feeling was that lawsuits of that type break down the bonds of society, and if that sort of thing was allowed to continue, no one would do anything for anybody else. And that, says JAPAN-THINK, is counterproductive.

· Dealing with Foreigners ·

And so, stepping into the tight little world of Japan, comes the American businessman. Hair combed, teeth polished, and suit crisped, the sheer energy and enthusiasm of the man more often than not blows away whoever is assigned from Japan to the first encounter. Friendship appears to be immediate, and straight talk on matters of business erupts within minutes of acquaintance. The problem, as the Japanese businessman is painfully aware, is that he has no real knowledge of specific business matters pertinent to the American—let alone authority to say more than "yes" or "no" on questions about the weather—because he was chosen for the first encounter as the result of a coin flip among those in the firm deemed to be able to speak passable English. Bluffing, all the way from the Hotel Okura to the office in a taxi, is more difficult in a second language than most people imagine. Of devastating effect is hearing himself referred to by his given name to his boss. The boss doesn't know that name, humiliation is complete, and it's only nine-thirty in the morning.

The American, meanwhile, is puzzled by an apparent lack of commitment on the part of his new friend. Sales estimates for the coming year were explained in detail during the cab ride to the office, and corporate profit estimates are confidentially revealed "just between you and me." It dawns on the American businessman that it really *does* take a long time to get a decision out of the Japanese, and at this rate a contract won't be signed until noon. (The American will still be harboring those same thoughts nine months later.)

Clearly, there are different concepts of *pace* and *content* when it comes to business discussions.

AMERI-THINK believes:
A. There is merit in "laying the cards on the table."
B. The direct approach cuts through unimportant side issues.
C. A one-on-one relationship with an executive of equal rank on the other side permits the working out of loose ends quickly and whenever necessary.

JAPAN-THINK believes:
A. The more people involved the better. It must be clear what's going on. More people mean more opinions, and these can be reviewed and discussed later.
B. Negotiation implies an element of give-and-take. There's no merit in "spilling guts" too early in the process.
C. The Village Elder must be protected through the advice and counsel of the others standing on the shore. Exposing him alone to the other side is unthinkable.

Seasoned Japanese executives know that Americans want agreements and action as quickly as possible. In order to do business, accommodations must be made. The Japanese accommodation is often made by assigning "advance troops" to research every aspect of people and products in the prospective trading partner before the first encounter.

Seasoned American executives know that concepts must be introduced at the appropriate level in a Japanese company and then there will be "dead time" while every single aspect of the proposal is mulled over by the horde. Knowing *when* to push for an answer is an art in itself, however. "Why," recently asked a Japanese businessman of an American one month into the dead time, "do you take so long to tell us final terms?"

· International Entertainment ·

International business intercourse means that opportunities abound for the pleasure/ordeal of international entertainment. AMERI-THINK considers it to be a social responsibility; JAPAN-THINK considers it to be essential if solid relationships are to be established. While the American hosts the visitor in his country with a round of golf, cocktails on the patio at the house, and dinner in the suburban "Surf 'n' Turf," and while the Japanese goes through the same motions in his country, the following precepts must be kept in mind by both sides.

JAPAN-THINK says:

A. Always bring gifts, hundreds of them, if not more. One can never be certain, from the cab driver to the American's executive secretary, who's going to be nice. Plus, who knows how many family members of hosts one will meet? Better double the number of gifts.

B. Be prepared to rave unabashedly at the size of everything. It will not be difficult when confronted with the servings of food (enough to feed a family of five in Japan) or the physical characteristics of domiciles (enough to *house* five families of five in Japan) but it may be a bit taxing when it comes to companies. Chase Manhattan would fit in a corner of Mitsubishi bank.

C. Praise all golf courses. They may be flat, long, and boring—without the nice little touches like greens perched on the sides of mountains, sheer cliffs on both sides of the fairways, and bunkers requiring rope-ladders for access—but the Americans like them. (But they certainly are long.)

D. Try to hold bowing in check. Americans don't do that. Washing hands after each new encounter is not done.

E. When in doubt, wear a blue suit and white shirt for all occasions (except golf), smoke only when no one's looking, and put the plastic thing hanging from a rod in the bathroom *inside* the tub before showering.

AMERI-THINK says:

A. Take a stab at eating things with chopsticks, that is, unless the food is really tasty. In those cases, a fork should be requested. Also don't be fooled by what Americans in America *think* is Japanese food. One will encounter some tofu and sushi in Japan, but the exotica of daily fare will be eye-opening. (Remember, Italians don't eat pizza and the Irish don't have corned beef all day long.) One needn't eat the eyes of the eels, or the gray/brown stuff inside the sea urchin. Wait until the cute little fish with whiskers stops moving before attempting to pick it up (with either the chopsticks or the fork).

B. Hitting a colleague over the head with a beer bottle during a "drinks with the staff" session after work is surprisingly counterproductive. Management techniques from America may not be fully appreciated at first, and the initial shipment of goods may not measure up to expectations (regardless of what is said in the contract), but physical mayhem is not the answer. It merely introduces another point of discussion in the orgy of meetings that must follow anything unexpected.

C. Do not fall in love with and propose marriage to the cute little thing wiping your forehead with a damp cloth, massaging the back of your neck, and rubbing the inside of your thigh at a hostess bar. She may really want you, with all her being, to step to the

microphone and sing "I Did It N
But remember, you are a pillar o.
and she's just doing her job.

D. Throwing up in public is "accepted" in Japa..
preferable, mind you, but given the crowds, it's or..
the only alternative. Being either the "thrower" or
"throwee" is equally important in relationship development.

E. When in doubt, wear a blue suit and white shirt for
all occasions (except while actually on the golf course,
otherwise to and fro . . .), leave blue jeans, Bermuda
shorts, and jogging sweats at home (unless running
around on the streets can be completed before dawn).
Smoke anywhere you want (even in the few "No
Smoking" areas) and be certain to wash yourself thoroughly and obviously on the little stool provided before entering the public bath. (You will be watched,
and nothing destroys relationships faster than leaping
directly from the eighteenth hole into a communal
rite of purification.)

· What's Fair? ·

Japan has come a long way since Jiro and his colleagues in
the village watched Commodore Perry's black ships arrive in
1853. The shock of it all was astounding. Japan had been
isolated for hundreds of years, had become inbred in its culture and beliefs, and had no real frame of reference in dealing
with the outside world. During the last 150 years, there have
been a half dozen or so isolated and previously unknown
tribes of people discovered in places like the Amazonian rain
forest and the jungles of New Guinea. And in effect, the
Japanese are one of those tribes.

Europe shed feudalism in the late middle ages—America never had it to shed. The Japanese have lived for only a few generations without the feudal structure in place—in fact, it wasn't until the land reforms after World War II that one of the bedrocks of the structure was eliminated.

In 1853 Japan had a rich tradition of cultural and artistic appreciation, but technologically it was not far removed from the Bronze Age. (The making of steel was understood, but it was officially discouraged. Without swords, the populace was easier to keep in line.) Trade and commerce were essentially an activity between and among villages with relatively simple needs. Concepts like "industrial revolution" could not even be imagined.

In addition, Japan never had the benefit (or curse) of organized religion to deal with. Shintoism is the official religion of Japan, but it is nothing like the Judeo-Christian organizations of the West. It is more a vague way-of-thought that recognizes an ongoing "spirit" of things Japanese—an ongoing spirit that continues forward and backwards through the generations. Right and wrong is not written down in a book somewhere, there are no commandments, and issues that Westerners consider "moral"—as the result of Judeo-Christian "teachings"—are mere pragmatic issues in a Japan accustomed to centuries of working and living together within a strong culture. "The Rules of the Game" evolved internally, not as the result of "outside" wisdom of the ages.

> AMERI-THINK (upon waking up with a new and different partner in bed): "I'm sorry about last night; it meant a lot to me."
> JAPAN-THINK (upon waking up with a new and different partner in bed): "Let's get out of here before somebody sees us."

The only way to catch up to the rest of the world was for Japan to make radical changes in the technological arena. When one stops to think about it, some of the bravest humans in recorded history were the Japanese sent abroad before the turn of the century for the purposes of bringing back scientific information and technological know-how. With their flowing robes and wooden sandals, they were not only stepping into different cultures in New York, London, Paris, and Berlin. They were stepping, because of their own peculiar time warp, into civilizations several centuries more advanced. ("Look at that, Jiro, the big metal building with smoke and steam coming out of it has wheels. And not only that, the wheels roll along those metal poles on the ground, and the whole thing can pull stuff behind it. They'll never believe *this* back in Kyoto.")

Humans are more "advanced" than animals in that animals must rely on inherent instinct for survival. A great deal of inefficient trial and error goes on before the rat in the maze makes it to the piece of cheese. Humans are able to learn specifics from each other—the first time around. And the Japanese learned very early on that the only way to survive now that they were exposed to the "outside" was to adapt—copy—technology and make it fit their own purposes. To start at square one would serve no purpose at all.

Here we are today, Japan technologically equal in most respects. Keep in mind, however, that people only several generations removed from feudalism are at the controls.

AMERI-THINK: "If we can get this little valve to open and close automatically, we can regulate the fuel in the rocket's second stage."
JAPAN-THINK: "Well, what do you know. Come back when you're finished, and I'll make it for you—better."

Chapter
7
· · ·

HERE COME THE KIDS

AMERI-THINK permits married couples to have children more or less at any time and in numbers approximately related to the economics available to support them. There are trends within trends, of course, and many couples postpone families in order to build up those economics. But, generally speaking, there's always room for one more tyke, and the soup can always be watered.

JAPAN-THINK knows that planning for children is the second most important thing a person must do in life. (Selecting a suitable employer is first.) The very real consideration of space, or lack thereof, must be taken into account. To introduce an infant into the family life of people dwelling in one or two small rooms is very difficult, for everyone involved. Seniority in the job must be piled up before income approaches that necessary for the next level of housing—three rooms. The average age of parents having their first child in Japan is 33 for the husband, 29.6 for the wife. The average number of children per family born since World War II is 2.9. The average number has dropped in the last five years—in 1990 it was 1.8.

AMERI-THINK believes that most children are cute, even, and up to a point, the ones whose diapers leak on your best suit. In fact, *anything* young and cuddly is cute—puppies, kittens, tree sloths, and teeny-weeny birdies. The emotions in the circumstances are universal. Cute does not go on forever, and each creature hits a stage when it is generally accepted that the puppy is really a pit-bull terrier, the kitten is a panther, and the birdie is a hawk. (Tree sloths *are* exceptions, but don't know it.) AMERI-THINK pegs the age for children to go from cute to "my little man" or "what a pretty young lady" at around four or five. (Younger in families with more than one child.)

JAPAN-THINK believes *all* children are cute—and in Japan they are. Round pudgy faces, rosy cheeks, page-boy haircuts—little kids resemble animated dolls. The difference in Japan is the "cute distinction" that is made based upon gender. Boys are permitted to stop being cute at around eight or nine. They still wear short pants to school and have the page-boy haircut, but gone are the Lord Fauntleroy collars and straw hats with chin straps. Once serious scabs and scars appear on elbows and knees, and when the cheeks unpudge, boys are allowed to be boys.

Girls in Japan, on the other hand, must continue to be cute until their first child is born. (There are exceptions to this; certain show business personalities must stay cute until grandmotherhood.) The flower of the fair sex maintains a little girl voice—with a lisp if possible—and a studied, giggling appearance of innocence well into her twenties. Men seem to like that. And yes, it does drive many young women up the wall, but one does what's expected of one.

AMERI-THINK considers formal education to start

around kindergarten age, although nursery schools do an expanding business each year. (The nursery schools exist partially to "prep" kids for kindergarten, and partially as a place to park them in two-job families.) The grade school years are relatively uneventful as are the high school years. Assuming the local school system is sound, and the student applies him or herself, the first element of trauma regarding subsequent education occurs late in senior high school when SAT scores and grade averages are sent off to college entrance officials. Unless one is shooting for one of the top-ten schools in the nation, most kids most of the time can matriculate at a university of choice. The ladder is long, but the rungs are evenly spaced.

JAPAN-THINK knows that "going to the right schools" is the ticket to phenomenal success and acclaim; anything less means a mediocre future. To graduate from one of the top three national universities, or to a slightly lesser extent from one of the top two private universities, means the future promise of a good job and many alternatives to select from in the matrimonial stakes. Graduates from Tokyo University, for example, hold most of the key positions in business and government, and upon retirement from those endeavors, consultancy options abound.

Whereas some 19 or 20 percent of Americans go on to higher education after high school, about 80 percent of Japanese do. And the first rung on the ladder is getting into the right nursery school, which feeds into the right kindergarten. Missing that rung may mean missing out on everything all the way up the line. ("Right" nursery schools typically accept one out of a dozen applicants, and in turn "right" kindergartens typically cut that number in half.) This means that the mother, from the time her child is aware of things and can put a round peg in a round hole, spends most of the child's waking life tutoring it in the clever little things nursery school operators look for during the admission process. ("Baby-sitters? No way. Who's going to teach flower drawing?")

To assist in the scramble up the ladder, at each rung along the way, are cram schools specializing in teaching the techniques and refinements of "test-taking." Virtually all academic students in Japan have spent time in cram schools, with the number of hours per week ranging from two to twenty. By the time college entrance exams roll around, high school students may spend as much as sixty hours per week slamming facts and figures into their brains. The rungs are pretty far apart at this stage—Tokyo University may accept three thousand or so students participating in the national exams. (There are close to a million students taking them each year.) Incidentally, once a student has been accepted into one of the top universities, the rungs on the ladder come close enough together to form a solid slide—into whatever choices await the plucky achiever. College life in Japan means sitting around in coffee shops, forming lifetime (and useful) friendships, participating in college recreational clubs, and now and then going to class.

JAPAN-THINK has based education primarily on the merits of rote memorization and repetition. Conceptual understanding, cognitive reasoning, and the practical application of learned facts and formulae tend not to receive much attention in the process. For example, Japanese students do very well in international tests of "math" ability at the high school level. In fact, the "math" in the tests is more accurately arithmetic—and Japanese students are arithmetically agile. Western countries (and, interestingly, China and India) produce many more true mathematicians per capita than Japan.

AMERI-THINK has based education primarily on individual achievement within a broad framework of deductive reasoning. At each step of the way, students are at least reminded of practical applications. The damn question about two trains approaching each other on the same track at different rates of speed, for example, teaches a practical application of arithmetic. American students tend to be taught problem-solving in this fashion; Japanese students are not. But if given the equation at the outset, a Japanese will "get the answer" while his American counterpart is still chewing on the end of his pencil. (The trains collided a mile from Pittsburgh, by the way.)

JAPAN-THINK places great value on conformity and adherence to group ideals in the education process. Students do not raise hands and ask for explanations if things whiz by them in class. Grades are generally not given on individual class participation. Grades are determined by written tests. All students throughout Japan at each level are essentially being taught the same things at the same time. A kid could move from Tokyo to Osaka, which often happens, and not lose a beat. Skipping a grade, or being held back, is practically unthinkable.

AMERI-THINK places greater emphasis on the give-and-take of classroom discussion. Although the general goal is to bring all students up to speed at more or less the same time, allowances for individual problems and achievements are made. And, of course, if deemed important some are asked to repeat a grade. Likewise, if some are exceptionally bright, emotionally mature, and bored out of their gourds, they may be advanced a grade.

A hypothetical conversation between an American and a Japanese student may run as follows:

AMERICAN STUDENT: "We have this pie here, and we ought to somehow divide it up equally for everybody."

JAPANESE STUDENT: "Euclid, circa 300 B.C., is the father of 'modern' geometry."

AMERICAN STUDENT: "Right. Maybe if we cut it from the center to the edge . . ."

JAPANESE STUDENT: "Pi, or 3.14159265, denotes the ratio of the circumference of a circle to its diameter."

AMERICAN STUDENT: "Right. But there are nine people and equal cuts create only eight pieces."

JAPANESE STUDENT: "Volume of a mass forms an indirect . . ."

AMERICAN STUDENT: "Hey, I've got it. Let's just take large spoonfuls and serve it in a pile."

JAPANESE STUDENT: "Right."

Chapter

8

. . .

GETTING ALONG ON A
DAY-BY-DAY BASIS

When it comes right down to it, just making it through the day is an achievement of some consequence. Arctic explorers and tax accountants can be justifiably proud of themselves if when crawling into bed they do so with the knowledge that they have at least not frozen to death or been thrown into jail. Sleep, as someone named Shakespeare once said, knits the raveled sleeve of care. And tomorrow, as someone named Scarlett once said, is another day. (Yesterday, as someone named McCartney once . . . never mind.)

Nine to five are the official working hours of most businesses in both Japan and the United States. But the number of real hours put in "on the job" is as different between the countries as the activities going on during those hours.

AMERI-THINK permits the worker to slink, scramble, or dash into the workplace and go immediately to his office or station. Conversation is rare and in fact can be dangerous during the first half hour ("Get stuffed, McGuire. I'll get to it after coffee"). The morning proceeds on a linear basis with paper moved from the IN to the OUT basket; phone calls received, answered, and made; meetings attended (during which facts are exchanged or status reports are made); and progress measured by increasing or diminishing piles of paper, ticks on a chart, or changes in numbers.

JAPAN-THINK sees the beginning of the workday as being the magic moment when all parts of the "group" reassemble into the natural order of things. Greetings are exchanged with co-workers, and a warm glow of satisfaction settles over everyone. Many companies in Japan reinforce the group feeling by staging calisthenics during the first fifteen minutes of the day. Everyone, from president to mailboy, stands at desk or work station and swings arms, does knee bends, and touches toes at the command of a voice from overhead speakers. It's the most natural thing in the world— everyone has been doing the same thing in a group since the first day of nursery school. (Imagine the scene, as observed in a modern steel-and-glass high-rise office building, from a building across the street. Each window "box" reveals a different section of a company—executives, clerical personnel, salesmen, maintenance staff—all swinging arms together on thirty of forty different floors. And even the latecomers, trust me, exit from elevators into the corridors swinging arms.)

The remainder of the morning in a Japanese office is a mix of paperwork and meetings, with meetings (of two, three, or a hundred people) taking up the lion's share of time. (It is a capital offense in Japan if green tea is *not* served during any and all gatherings of two or more bodies.)

AMERI-THINK considers lunchtime to be an opportunity for businessmen and women to work on necessary relationships in their jobs. Anyone with "business" outside the four walls of the building—and this means just about everyone except clerical staff—goes out to confirm deals, open negotiations, gather information from competitors, or have a drink or two with co-workers who are otherwise inaccessible in the office. By and large it is productive time, but nothing ever gets cranked up again and running at full speed in the office until after two o'clock.

JAPAN-THINK considers lunchtime to be a period for refueling. About half of all salarymen and women in Japan eat lunch in the office—either at their desks (surrounded by others doing the same thing) or in company cafeterias. Those who do go outside at lunch do so in the company of three or four co-workers. Food is gobbled at alarming speed, and everyone is more or less ready to go back to work in forty-five minutes. Japanese executives *are* seen dining at lunchtime in the more relaxed ambience of hotels or major restaurants, but as often as not they will be in the company of non-Japanese executives—usually Americans.

AMERI-THINK considers the afternoon to be an extension of the morning—more linear task work. By the time five o'clock rolls around, a great deal has been accomplished. Problems have been solved, deals have been concluded, and a great deal of paperwork has been processed through the system. Individual decisions, big or small, have been made all along the way. Within an hour of five most offices will be empty.

JAPAN-THINK thinks of the afternoon as the time to go out and confirm deals, open negotiations, or gather information from competitors. These tasks are usually assigned to the younger cadre of salarymen, and the venue for their meetings is the thousands of coffee and tea shops in and around all business areas. "Afternoon" meetings in Japan usually don't begin until five, when everyone gets back to the office. At this time, information gained during the day or developments arising from previous activities are reviewed and dissected by everyone with remote involvement. At six o'clock there is still a full complement of staff on hand in the office, but the ranks begin to thin at six-thirty. It is at this time that most paperwork is done. The more meetings a person has attended during the day means the more paperwork there is left over in the evening. It is, therefore, something of a badge of honor to be swamped in documents at seven. Less-important people, like the clerical staff, weren't required at all the meetings.

Leaving the office in America requires one to say "Good night" or "See you tomorrow." Leaving the office in Japan is a procedure requiring exquisite timing and style. Generally speaking, no one should leave before his or her boss. But since everyone in a corporation has a boss, except the chairman, no one moves until something happens way up the line. Because chairmen could die in their chairs (thereby trapping everybody for an eternity of twenty-four-hour paper-shuffling), elaborate rituals have been developed to break up the work force at the end of the day. A supervisor will remember an urgent appointment for drinks with a supplier, a department head will discover tickets to the ballet in his wallet, a section chief will receive a call from a dying mother. Pretty soon, it's "okay" to split. Most Japanese offices are empty by 10:00 P.M.

Pressures take separate forms in the two cultures. In both cases, the problems in dealing with people—both inside and outside the company—top the list. But in AMERI-THINK, "doing the job" is more transaction-oriented, and in disputes on "people" matters the American worker can always point to specific accomplishments in the form of sales figures, expense reductions, or widgets produced as a defense. In Japan, a worker could go weeks, months, or even years doing his job but without being required to make a single individual decision or being asked to take responsibility for a specific project. (An interesting exercise is to ask groups of American and Japanese workers to quantify on a percentage basis their personal contribution to a specific project. The totals will always be more than one hundred for Americans—less than one hundred for Japanese.) JAPAN-THINK places more emphasis on "people skills" and being able to work within the group. When there are problems in these areas, the frustrated Japanese employee has nothing to fall back on.

Which way of work is more efficient? Well, they can't really be compared—it's the apples and oranges thing. If "efficient" means getting tasks done in a short time, then the Americans are more efficient. If "efficient" means making certain everyone knows what's going on so as to avoid future screw-ups, then the Japanese are more efficient.

An American executive visiting Japan will say that the "work" being done could be accomplished between nine and five. A lot of time is wasted in meetings, miniature social gatherings, and staring out windows.

A Japanese executive visiting America will say that everyone seems to work in little cells, and the left hand (to coin a phrase) doesn't know what the right hand is doing.

· Ladies' Day ·

Getting working husbands up and out of the house is the chore of all housewives. For the American housewife, it means turning on the automatic coffeemaker. For the Japanese housewife, it means turning on the automatic rice cooker. While an American husband might be inclined to go into the kitchen and slice a grapefruit or pour a bowl of cereal, a Japanese husband wouldn't dream of approaching that area of the house. A typical breakfast for him might be rice, salted fish, tossed salad, and tea. It wouldn't occur to him to learn how to arrange that on his own.

Children in the family make the "getting out of the house"

process a little more complicated, particularly in American households. Husbands and children tend to leave the house at about the same time. In Japanese households, husbands leave an hour or two before the children, with the result being that the Japanese housewife doesn't have to deal with the "crisis hour" when everyone leaves at once. Instead, the process is longer, more drawn out (and probably more exhausting).

Once all of that happens, Japanese housewives have much in common with their American sisters. They do more things as individuals than their husbands (who are off to group battles).

Straightening up the house is a pain in the neck in both cultures. AMERI-THINK is firmly committed to the principle "Cleanliness is next to Godliness." This means all flat surfaces must be washed, scrubbed, or vacuumed on a regular basis. (Vacuuming an American house can sometimes seem to be not unlike plowing a forty-acre field.) Kitchens look like display models in department stores in that all the equipment is there (pots and pans hanging on the wall, spice racks on the counter), but it's not clear if anyone has ever actually *cooked* there. (Now and then a cornflake can be found in the corner on the floor, but except for the Gary Larson cartoons taped to the refrigerator door, very few signs of life exist.) All the polishing and neatness is appreciated, but it certainly is hard work.

JAPAN-THINK appreciates cleanliness, but different problems face the housewife. "Putting things back in place" is her obsession. Visualize a family of four living in a total space about the size of a typical American master bedroom plus perhaps a room the size of a den. All the accoutrements of family life—television sets, stereos, books, clothes, toys, chairs, tables, kitchen ware, sports equipment, decorative knickknacks, awkward gifts from rich uncles, souvenirs brought back from Hawaii—have to be *put* somewhere. (One space-saving custom remains in most families. Instead of beds, people sleep on cushions called futons placed on the floor at night. But of course, *they* have to be rolled up and put somewhere during the day.)

Japanese kitchens—which Americans would probably call "kitchenettes"—are very clearly and obviously "work stations." There is very little space, no pantries, and so all the things that don't fit into the one or two cupboards are out in the open. (Just for the fun of it, American housewives might try this: Take everything out of all cupboards, pantries, and food closets, rope off two-thirds of your kitchen, and into the remaining third place everything you own that has to do with cooking or eating. It won't be quite the same—American kitchens, even one-third of them, have larger counter areas. Also Japanese tend to use more individual plates, dishes, and bowls per meal. But you'll begin to appreciate the Japanese housewife's task in "tidying up.")

While the American housewife is vacuuming the "south forty," loads of laundry can be run through the washer/dryer process. While the Japanese housewife is squeezing things into cracks and crannies (or piling things on shelves that run to the ceiling), she's also doing laundry—but only the wash. Most Japanese homes have a washer—smaller, with the capacity of about two pails—but custom (and again, space considerations) makes "natural" drying preferable. Things are hung up to dry in front of open windows or on the small balconies outside most apartments. (Unless it's raining, futons are also hung out the window each day. "Fresh air is good for them," and it solves one problem in the space game.)

People don't wear shoes in Japanese houses. If a Japanese housewife has a vacuum cleaner, it is one usually the size of those that are plugged into the cigarette lighter to clean the floor of the car. A dustpan and brush suffice otherwise.

AMERI-THINK knows that buying goods in large volume or quantity is usually more economical than picking up little packages of the same things. An American housewife can hit the supermarket once or twice a week, load up the station wagon, and go home with the knowledge that she probably paid as low a price on a retail basis as possible. (Supermarkets in America operate on surprisingly low margins.)

JAPAN-THINK appreciates the economics of all that, but where on earth would one put a "giant economy size" box of cornflakes or one of those massive bags of Ken-L-Ration dog food? Someone would have to move out of the apartment to make space for all that economy. The Japanese housewife, therefore, goes shopping at least every other day, if not once a day. Because of the custom of shopping daily, less frozen or canned food is purchased—Japanese tend to eat only fresh vegetables and fruit which is delivered daily to the stores. And because the stores themselves are small, the shelf life of goods is short. Very few products like bread or potato chips have preservatives. Only a short time elapses between manufacture and consumer purchase. The down side, of course, is that things get stale in forty-eight hours—less during the Rainy Season.

Both American and Japanese housewives with young children are bound to them and the house when the school day ends. Japanese housewives *without* children have a number of options available to them during the day. Once the individual effort of housecleaning and shopping is finished, the group beckons with a myriad of organized activities planned and arranged by neighborhood associations, ward offices, city governments, private athletic or health clubs, or school alumnae groups. ("Wards" are subgovernment entities within a city, and they provide, among other things, athletic facilities in the form of gymnasiums, swimming pools, social centers,

tennis courts, etc., for people living within their boundaries.)
One ward in Tokyo lists the following *team* activities open to
women.

1. Volleyball
2. Basketball
3. Gateball (a form of croquet—usually played by senior
   citizens)
4. Tug-of-War
5. Synchronized swimming
6. Water polo
7. Softball
8. Field hockey

In addition to the above, the following *social* activities are
listed.

1. Mah-jongg
2. Bridge
3. Swimming
4. Tennis
5. Golf (driving only)
6. Flower arranging
7. Sumi-e painting
8. Kimono wearing (This actually is a course in putting
   one on—more difficult, it would appear, than one
   might think.)
9. Cooking (Japanese)
10. Cooking (Chinese)
11. Cooking (French)
12. Cooking (Western)
13. Exercise and aerobics (and not a moment too soon,
    after all that eating)

Multiply the above by the other half dozen organizations or so that are available to the housewife, and one begins to appreciate how organized things are in Japan. (But remember, it's the natural way of things, and it always has been. Jiro's wife was preparing to join the other ladies in the village for something or other when Perry's black ships arrived.)

Chapter

9

. . .

LET'S EAT

It could be argued that the greatest experiments in human history are not in the areas of science, technology, or social organization. They are, instead, in the area of putting things in the mouth, chewing, and swallowing.

Grinding stuff up with our teeth and committing the bits to our stomachs is a process we call "eating," and it has apparently been going on for a long time. (And, if we believe all grandmothers, we *are* what we eat.)

But can one even imagine what went through the mind of the brave pioneer to prompt him, to the astonishment of his pals sitting around the cave, to get up, walk over to the hairy-thing-that-goes-moo, squeeze the little tubes hanging down from the bag between its hind legs, and *drink* what came out?

Imagine the guy who, probably on a dare, walked over

to the feathered-thing-that-flies-and-goes-cluck, picked up the hard-white-thing-that-comes-out-its-rear-end and put the insides into his mouth! ("Hey, let's try scrambling it on a hot rock.").

Or consider the first person to speculatively eye the little oink-doggy-with-no-hair-but-a-curly-tail . . . well, you know. The point is that we owe a lot to these gentlemen (or ladies)— the bacon and eggs were excellent this morning—but their genius was probably not even recognized at first. Perhaps a moment of silence in their memory . . . Okay, where were we?

Ah, food. Americans, composed of people from everywhere, are surprisingly timid eaters. One would think that with all the different cultures brought to the country down through the years, with the accompanying dietary specialties, there'd be more adventure in the air. Consider the following:

1. Chicken Kiev
2. Chicken Curry
3. Chicken Stew (with dumplings)
4. Chicken and Avocado Casserole
5. Chicken Tetrazzini
6. Chicken Creole Gumbo
7. Chicken Fricassee
8. Chicken Pie
9. Chicken Milanese
10. Chicken à la King
11. Chicken Cacciatore
12. Chicken Fried Like They Do in Kentucky
13. Chicken (Stuffed)

Now there's a pretty broad range of cultural heritages represented in the above list, but the astute reader may notice a common thread running through the menus. Exotic as it all may seem, we're still talking, ah, chicken.

Japanese, on the other hand, will eat anything that either was, or is, alive. This includes all the different types of flora *and* fauna on the planet. ("Weasel innards and catalpa tree leaves? Mmmm, could be good with soy sauce.")

The only reason anyone can give for this is the relatively poor, in fact in many areas mere subsistence-type diets the Japanese had to live with for centuries. Isolated by both topography and government decree—people are easier to control if they don't band together—villagers depended almost entirely on whatever raw food possibilities existed in the immediate area. Rice was always the main crop, and it was mixed with whatever was either handy or happened to grow well locally. Fishermen in the north ate whale meat, salmon, and a type of sweet potato. Fishermen in the south ate shellfish and whatever came in with their nets. People in the relatively few sections of flat land ate eels from the rivers and gourds. People in the mountains never even saw fish (unless a wandering outcast happened their way with salted fish) and relied on hunting game and small animals instead. Here and there particularly isolated villagers domesticated fowl and occasionally cattle, but these were exceptions. There was no tradition of "market towns" with farmers coming in from all over to sell or trade merchandise and food. Local people ate local food.

In the last 150 years, people have mixed throughout the islands of Japan—all bringing to the common pool a plethora of "favorite" local dishes and foods. Most of those foods are in the fish and vegetable categories, and compared to the relatively few alternatives in a Westerner's staple—meat— fish and vegetables provide hundreds of alternatives.

"And what are these little things?"

"Braised fish brains wrapped in mountain weeds. My grandmother used to make them."

"Oh, yummy."

Now then, let's compare typical daily diets of average Americans and average Japanese.

Ameri-Think:

Breakfast
Cornflakes, Sugar Pops, Cheerios, or bran stuff
Bacon and eggs and toast, or bagels and lox
Grapefruit or some kind of juice

Lunch
Cheeseburger with fries, chicken noodle soup with crackers, hot beef sandwich with mashed potatoes, or bagels and lox

Dinner
Meat, potatoes, corn if you're lucky—broccoli if you're not
Apple pie

Random Snacks
Pizza, potato chips, pretzels, peanuts, bagels and lox, either an apple or banana

Japan-Think:

Breakfast
Salted fish, pickled cucumbers and radishes, raw egg, tossed salad, bean curd soup with miniature clams on the

half-shell, salmon custard, sea slug stew, fishcakes, sweet-potato paste, gladiola bulbs, rice, green tea

Lunch
Curry rice, sushi, curry rice, baked pork and eggs, curry rice, fried eels and soy sauce, curry rice, fried noodles, curry rice, fish cakes, curry rice, fisherman's surprise, curry rice, bamboo shoots and spinach, curry rice, cole slaw with soy sauce, curry rice, dumplings with sweet bean paste (stuffed), curry rice, or McDonald's hamburgers

Dinner
See *Lunch* (above) but substitute baked squid, Kobe beef, chicken on a stick, tofu pie, fish stew, roasted squash, white asparagas wrapped in seaweed, and more salted fish for curry rice.

Snacks
Pizza, dried squid, rice crackers, boiled soybeans in the shells, beef jerky, candied peanuts, even more salted fish

The life expectancy in 1930 (when retirement ages were pegged at fifty-five) was fifty-seven for Japanese males, fifty-nine for Japanese females. Today Japan has the longest life expectancy of any nation on earth—79.4 for males, 83.3 for females. Some maintain that the introduction of meat and other Western foods to the diet (dairy products, wheat, and grains other than rice) is responsible. The Western diet is perhaps partially responsible for the increasing size of individual Japanese each generation, but it is also probably a factor in elevated cholesterol levels and weight problems Japanese are now beginning to experience.

In fact, the pooling of traditional *Japanese* foods from all the different regions of the country now provides everyone with a broad and reasonably balanced range of items from which to choose. And looking at the items, it's pretty healthy stuff.

The problem is, for the healthy stuff to work one must put it in the mouth, chew, and swallow it.

10

. . .

ILLICIT SEX, PORNOGRAPHY, AND ALL THE THINGS THAT ARE FUN TO READ ABOUT PROVIDED NO ONE'S LOOKING OVER YOUR SHOULDER

This is a touchy subject. (See Chapter 12.)

11

. . .

GOVERNMENT, INDUSTRY, EMPLOYEES: MAKING IT ALL WORK

Japan was physically and economically devastated at the end of World War II. About 25 percent of all housing was destroyed, and in cities like Tokyo over half the population was homeless. Factories lay in ruins, and the infrastructure for delivering the basic services of food, water, and clothing was in a shambles. Acute inflation set in, and even if some goods were available, they often were beyond the reach of the man literally on the street. Black market businesses flourished as they provided the only practical method of delivery and distribution of food, clothing, salt, and soap.

People squatted where they were and eventually rebuilt homes from scraps obtained from the ruins of bombed sites. This, incidentally, contributed to the hodgepodge of architecture and the labyrinth of today's road system in places like Tokyo.

In addition to the physical and economic destruction, there was an additional burden in the hearts and minds of

Japanese. The realization that the emperor was fallible and not the unerring high authority everyone had come to believe him to be was a tremendous blow to the citizenry. (As a point of interest, Westerners believed that the Japanese believed the emperor to be "God." The problem with the belief of that belief is that Westerners have a traditional and religious definition of Him—which is decidedly lofty and supernatural. The Japanese, and it should come as no surprise by now, think of things differently. Although atrocities were committed in the emperor's name, he was a "god" only in the sense that he was the highest of the high authorities reaching toward the heavens in an essentially feudalistic society. That put him pretty far up there, and way beyond the unquestioning man on the street—now homeless. But whether or not he was really descended from a bolt of lightning, a pigeon, or a golden canoe wreathed in flowers was never a debatable issue. All anyone knew for sure was that "the boss" blew it, and for a society accustomed to following the leader, that's bad enough.)

Despite the destruction of World War II (or, as some have whispered, *because* of the destruction), Japan was forced to pull itself up by the sandal straps and work with absolute dedication to rebuild everything and catch up once again from ground zero. (The whisperers maintain that the process was easier because old institutions did not have to be dismantled and blended into the new order.)

A constitution was overlaid on the citizenry by the American Occupation, but everyone was too involved in the business of survival for the niceties of the concept to be fully appreciated. At least the emperor wasn't executed (some bad guys were); "now let's get going."

· Government and Industry ·

If it had not been for the Japanese tendency to think and work together as a group (remember, no one raises hands in class and wants an individual explanation of what's going on—following the Japanese maxim that "the nail that stands out gets pounded down"), and the tendency to develop fierce loyalty to country and employer, the "Japanese Miracle" of the last half century would not have happened.

AMERI-THINK believes in individual initiative and freedom from government interference. "It's none of the government's business what we charge for air fares," for example, or "Survival of the fittest is what counts."

JAPAN-THINK knows "We're all in this together, so what action produces the maximum benefit for the maximum *of us?*" (Japanese would consider mass suicide off Mt. Fuji before toying with deregulation of the savings and loan industry. Benefits and security for the maximum would be difficult to demonstrate.)

Cooperation between business and government has been crucial to Japan's successes in the last century. But it's fair to say that it is easier for Japan in this regard than it is for Americans. Early in the reconstruction period after the war, government and industry forged an alliance—supported by the populace—to aggressively fight for economic development. It was a very basic matter of survival, something with which Americans were not faced. Cooperation at all levels of society—a phenomenon comfortable to the Japanese—was and still is the keystone.

There are tradeoffs, however. Japan is almost homogeneous, but not quite. The people having difficulty marrying outside their ranks, for example, are not really considered "pure" Japanese. "Guest workers" from elsewhere in Asia and temporarily residing Western executives are clearly *gai-*

jin, or outsiders. Japanese women, in government or industry, typically get the short end of the stick (but for one reason or another have accepted that situation). What remains is a great mass of people all thinking and behaving alike. And the very best go into government administration or business.

AMERI-THINK: "We *do not* discriminate in government hiring practices."

JAPAN-THINK: "We *do* discriminate in government hiring practices."

Japan does not really deal with minority rights and interests, redressing wrongs from the past, equality of "opportunity," nondiscrimination on a racial or sexual basis, and all the other issues facing a complex society like America. The "minorities" are small, and that's tough. "They will indirectly share in the spoils." In 1991 the Japanese government made a very fundamental decision—something South Koreans have been agitating for since a great number of them were dragooned into forced slave labor in Japan during the 1920s and 1930s—and that is the cancellation of regularly fingerprinting them as aliens. (It is humiliating for second- and third-generation residents who wouldn't know a word of Korean if you put flames to their feet.) SOUTH KOREAN FINGER-PRINTING LAW TO BE ABOLISHED screamed the headlines. If a similar decision were made in America, the new procedure could be put in place along about Tuesday afternoon. In Japan the bureaucrats (the best of the best) need more time to digest this radical departure from "things as they should be." The new law goes into effect, so that "bureaucracy can adjust," one year and 361 days from its proclamation. And who said it was easy dealing with the Japanese from the outside?

The cooperation between government and industry takes many forms. The tax system is designed to encourage private investment by granting hefty depreciation allowances. The basic infrastructure in the country was rebuilt by the government in cooperation with and for the benefit of industry to improve its ability to produce. (Personal savings were encouraged by lowering tax rates on interest and dividends. Remember, the average Japanese puts money in the bank instead of into individual home ownership.)

The development of new industries is actively encouraged by the government at the same time it is giving assistance to existing industries. In the insurance industry, for example, there are twenty-three property and casualty companies (compared to several thousand in America). The Ministry of Finance regulates the companies (as opposed to the American system wherein each of the fifty states regulates only the companies headquartered in its state), and the thrust of the regulation is both to protect the smaller companies from the larger companies, and to protect *all* the insurance companies from outside (non-Japanese) companies. This is done by closely scrutinizing new concepts in insurance coverage to make certain everyone has the underwriting skills and claim payment ability before approving the policy forms and releasing them to all companies at once. Anything not thoroughly understood by everyone in all twenty-three companies never sees the light of day. This is particularly true when the new concept is introduced by a non-Japanese company. Competitive advantage is gained only through service or the establishment of relationships with the large industrial groups (and the cooperation of the ministry, of course). The same is true in banking and financial services, where rigid controls are maintained over foreign exchange, trading, investment funds, and other instrument transfers.

Given the tremendous growth of the Gross National Income since August 1945, it's difficult to argue that anything *but* the close cooperation of government and industry would have worked for Japan. "Success" makes debate moot.

· Employers and Employees ·

There is a theory, which sounds so neat it can't be true, that the difference in American and Japanese attitudes toward work springs from the difference between a "hunter/gatherer" ancestry and a "rice culture" ancestry. Americans are descended from a primitive life-style where the emphasis for survival purposes was on individual initiative. Hunters would go off by themselves and chase woolly bison over the horizon. Winners—those succeeding in that little chore—flourished. Losers starved. The Japanese, on the other hand, are descended from a primitive life-style where the emphasis was on cooperation and harmony (growing rice), and individual attitudes were counterproductive to the requirements of survival. ("Jiro, if you say one more word about going off and chasing woolly bison over the horizon, you're history. Besides, what *are* woolly bison?")

Whether or not one accepts the theory is not important. However, it must be said that the Japanese *were* living until early this century in a culture not too far removed from the earliest (and primitive) rice cultures. On the Western side, a lot has happened since the last woolly bison disappeared over the horizon—the development of complex agricultural societies and the industrial revolution, to name but two. However, consider the individual initiative it took to go to America in the first place, and then expand across the continent and settle it. (Interestingly, Americans did go off by themselves, stake out farming territory, and plop themselves alone and in the middle of their land. The Europeans tended to gravitate toward the establishment of cooperative villages, with farmland radiating out from a central location. To be alone means to be self-reliant—a characteristic of individualism.)

If one were to shake an American awake in the middle of the night and ask what "rights" mean, he would say they were something belonging to *him* ("and get the hell out of my bedroom"). A Japanese shaken awake would respond that "rights" were something belonging to *us* ("and are you asking everyone the same question?").

For whatever reason, Japanese are willing, eager, capable of, and comfortable with "working together." The more doing it, and the closer together they are when it's being done, the better. Everything, from historical development to cultural conditioning, the requirements of surviving in very little space, the thrust of educational policies, and the similar concerns and interests of a nearly homogeneous people, have *conditioned* the Japanese to work together. (And transferring Japanese "management techniques" en bloc to America—no matter how thoroughly the text is studied—won't work. The instinct isn't there.)

Decision-making

AMERI-THINK: The boss calls together his key staff and announces that everyone has stopped buying their widgets. "How do we get people to buy them again?" he asks. The question is kicked around for hours, days, maybe even weeks. "Make them bigger," say some; "Make them smaller," say others. The sales manager wants them "cheaper," the chief accountant wants them "more expensive." "Prettier," chimes in the head of advertising from the far end of the table. Arguments are presented by each of the specialists in his or her field—individual career paths could be at stake—and finally the boss bangs the gavel on the desk. "Bigger *and* prettier," is the decision. There are risks, and heads could roll if things go wrong, but what is life but a sequence of risks?

JAPAN-THINK: The boss calls together his key staff, who in turn bring in *their* key staff, and announces that everyone has stopped buying their widgets. Into the stunned silence, the man in charge of the widget division apologizes profusely, states that he "did his best," and offers to commit suicide right there and then on the spot. That ritual completed (and it rarely involves actual suicide), the issue is tackled. You will note that the boss didn't even ask "how to get people to buy them again." He just stated a fact.

The discussion goes on for hours. Each person in the room makes a very careful statement apropos the problem, but reveals very little of his own beliefs on the matter. There's no sense doing that too soon, and until everyone's feelings emerge, there is always the risk of stepping on toes and sensitivities. The boss needn't even remain awake during this stage of the deliberation.

A consensus will never be reached at the first meeting, and things break up so that little groups of people can meet informally—often involving additional staff members—and *define the problem.* At this stage, it is important to understand that all employees at all levels of the company are very well trained, have taken many company-sponsored courses on the business of their particular company, and are on career paths that may have them working in a dozen different departments down through the years. (Oil companies, for example, regularly assign *all* new employees, young men *and* women, to spend time in the stations pumping gas.)

It takes quite a while by Western standards (during which time Western stockholders would be up in arms over the problems in the widget business), but after a series of meetings—which may include several times the number attending the first meeting—agreement on a course of action is reached. All opinions from all sources have been reviewed, revised, eliminated, enhanced, or whatever, and there is now no doubt in anyone's mind what must be done. Everyone *may* agree that the problem is widgets, and to sell more they have to be bigger and prettier. But since that question wasn't even asked by the boss, as much time was spent "defining the problem" as was spent on anything else. What may happen, and this has worked very well for Japan, is that it is decided that the widgets *are* the problem, and the company should stop making them. Instead, add a doodad here, remove a thingamajig there, and we are now in the . . . GADGET business! (And those gadgets proceed to blow the socks off competitors around the world.)

Implementation

AMERI-THINK recognizes implementation as being one of management's more difficult tasks. Decisions from "on high" must be explained and explained at level after level. Opinions will vary as to the wisdom of all this, and memo rockets will shoot back up the chain of command pointing out difficulties in the "manufacturing sector" which were not even considered. Additionally, union members must be placated and unanticipated compromises might have to be made just to get off square one. And even if the Americans, in their fashion, do hit upon the "gadget" idea, it could take months to get the thingamajig supplier to stop making them and tool up instead for doodads—the guy in charge of communicating this may not know what the hell is going on.

JAPAN-THINK knows that "implementation" is merely a matter of pushing a button. Implementers are in on the game.

There obviously are strengths and weaknesses in both the Japanese and American systems. For the Americans, the speed of the decision-making process puts them one jump ahead. But if at the end of the day the total time for decision-making and implementation is the same, the advantage is lost. Because decisions must be made at an increasing pace, the Japanese system is slowly being modified so that information and feedback at all levels of the company can be transmitted quicker. In this regard, advances in communication technology are improving the system every day.

A point to ponder: an industrial saboteur in America would toss a monkey wrench into the works. An industrial saboteur in Japan would toss a bogus *idea* into the works. (But remember, it is much more costly to turn things around if things get as far as the implementation stage.)

· Unions ·

If one were to return to the room of the sleeping American, wake him up again and ask what he did for a living, he would reply with a description of *his* job—steamfitter, accountant, astronaut, salesman, homicidal maniac. ("Stop right there, four-eyes, and I'll *show* you what I do for a living.") Awakening the same Japanese, he would answer—after apologizing for falling asleep in the interim—by stating the name of his company. ("I'm with Mitsubishi.") the fact that he is an engineer, architect, or chauffeur would come out only after further questioning.

Workers organized on a *trade* basis is a centuries-old idea in the Western world. Artisans and craftsmen, proving themselves in the apprentice system, would go from job site to job site working on projects and policing themselves on both skill levels and performance standards. The industrial revolution changed things in that the craftsmen could stay in one place and work instead of roaming around the countryside looking for a new cathedral to build. The trade organization became part of the industrial organization.

In Japan there was only one employer, and that was either the village headman, or *daimyo,* or the shogun. Loyalties and commitment were organized vertically. The important relationships are the ones involving employment. As you'll recall, even the seating arrangements at weddings reflect this, with the employers getting the good seats up front or at the head table.

Although there are exceptions, the union movement in Japan is organized primarily on a *company* basis, not a *trade* basis. And the companies that have unions are about half the companies in the minority of firms employing one hundred or more people. (Ninety-four percent of all companies in Japan have *fewer than* one hundred employees—and they rarely have unions. "There's no point," it is said.)

Company unions serve several purposes, not the least of which is providing a framework for labor/management negotiations at salary increase and bonus times. Generally speaking, increases and promotions are announced once a year in big companies—usually in the spring—after the performance of the company during the past year is thoroughly analyzed. Workers expect to share in the spoils and, subject to government guidelines (in an attempt to control inflation) in each type of industry, the spoils are shared. Hammering out agreements is a long and difficult process, but at least the hammerers on both sides each have a pretty good idea of what's fair and what the company can afford.

If things seem to stall at the hammering stage, unions provide another framework for blowing off steam. Under controlled circumstances, mind you, employees may take to wearing red armbands in the office (which say things like "fight hard" or "together we win.") If an agreement on wage and bonus levels is still stalled, the union may take the next step of selecting one evening each week—let's say Thursday evening—and sending a committee around to each work station in the company at about five-thirty to chant "Go home" once or twice. Some people actually do leave the office—less than half as a rule—but the majority hangs in there piling up overtime hours. In the relatively rare case where all this radical behavior doesn't seem to be getting anywhere, the employees may take to the streets in front of their office buildings and, armbands supplemented by red headbands, shout slogans and pass out handbills to passersby. (Interestingly, this activity takes place on *their* lunch hour—employees go back to their desks as soon as the lunch period is finished.) It is very rare for an actual work stoppage to occur. The hammerers do finally get to the compromise stage before things really get out of hand.

There are various schools of thought about the company union phenomenon in Japan. Wearing headbands and shouting in the street seems to belie the impression that all of Japan is one big happy family all striving for common goals. Yet the concept *does* provide the safety valve for blowing off steam (and frustrations *do* occur in the work force). And in another sense, the activity of a company union is really a "unifying" force among employees. (Many companies encourage what would otherwise be considered "middle management" people to be part of the company union—older and wiser heads keep things in check.) Anything that unifies in Japan is ultimately good.

A final note on cooperation between employers and employees has to do with the "bonus system." Leaping as they did from a rice-culture agricultural society to an advanced industrial culture in less than a century, some old practices linger among the Japanese. In the countryside, when the crops come in there's cash in the bank. (It is then parceled out carefully until the crops come in again.) After the war, when cash was scarce and industry was rebuilding, a compromise was hit upon that "carried on" the old traditions. "Bonuses" are paid to today's Japanese twice a year—once in the spring and once at the end of the year. As much as 40 percent of annual employee income is represented by these bonuses, and the amount is guaranteed. About one-third of the amount is paid in the spring; the bulk is paid at the end of the year. Examined closely, the employers are getting away with deferred payment of operating expenses.

AMERI-THINK: "Hey, that's *my* money you're hanging on to and paying me on an interest-free basis."

JAPAN-THINK: "It's okay, it helps me save."

And save they do. Or purchase great portions of Manhattan island.

Chapter
12
· · ·

ILLICIT SEX, PORNOGRAPHY, AND ALL THE THINGS THAT ARE FUN TO READ ABOUT PROVIDED NO ONE'S LOOKING OVER YOUR SHOULDER: PART II

The more said about this the better.

God created Adam. Watching His handiwork wander around lost for most of the day, refusing to eat his vegetables, and tracking mud from his bare feet into the house, God decided upon a refinement in the grand scheme of things. Whilst Adam dozed—sorry, ladies, this is how it was explained to me—God plucked a rib from Adam's side and fashioned a helpmate named Eve.

So far, so good.

Adam and Eve frolicked happily and innocently like pre-1988 yuppies on vacation, when it occurred to God to issue one set of instructions to the pair. Did He discuss the dangers of buying long and selling short? Did He discuss the stress of wintering in Cleveland? Did He discuss a method for selecting Vice-Presidential candidates? No sir, He did not. In-

stead. He pointed to a tree in the middle of the garden—a
tree like all the others, but maybe even a little better—and
said, and I quote, "DO NOT, I REPEAT, DO NOT, WHATEVER
YOU DO, DO NOT EAT THE SWEET, SUCCULENT FRUIT FROM
THIS VERY, VERY SPECIAL TREE WHATEVER YOU DO. THE
FRUIT IS SO GOOD IT WILL MAKE YOUR HEAD SPIN. SO DO
NOT, I REPEAT, DO NOT EAT IT. DO I MAKE MYSELF PER-
FECTLY CLEAR? DO NOT EAT THE FRUIT FROM THIS WON-
DERFUL TREE."

So far still good.

Adam and Eve continued frolicking without a care in the
world (and in a manner which we who know the rest of the
story can only imagine) until that fateful day Eve wandered
over by The Tree. The sun was bright, the grass was warm,
and there wasn't a cloud in the sky. Adam was over amongst
the daffodils practicing the multiplication tables.

Lucifer, whose habit it was to dress up in funny costumes—sometimes as a London bobby, sometimes as an
American football player, and sometimes as a 1920s flapper—
had that very day selected a snake costume.

"Pssst [or more accurately, "hssst"]," he said to Eve.

"What ho?" said Eve, tossing her golden curls over her
shoulder. "What are you doing up in the very, very special
tree?"

"Having the time of my life," replied Lucifer. "And it's
all because of these wonderful apples," he added.

"But . . ."

"No 'buts' about it," interrupted Lucifer. "Just one of
these apples, and you'll know as much about things as the
Voice in the Sky."

"But . . ."

"You argue eloquently, my sweet young thing, yet to no
avail. Eat one of these," urged Lucifer. "Trust me," he added
for good measure.

It is not important to dwell upon what happened next, other than to report that Adam, still puzzling over the eleven-by-twelve answer, took a bite of the apple Eve gave him. ("If you don't, I swear, Adam, I'm not frolicking tomorrow.")

What *is* important is to touch briefly on the consequences of this misadventure. First of all, God threw Adam and Eve out of the garden. That certainly was His right, after all it was His garden, and I think everyone will agree His instructions were pretty explicit. He then condemned them and theirs to a lifetime of scratching and eking out a living (which seems so natural it's difficult to comment upon it). But the bit about Adam and Eve being forever clouded by shame as a result of the original sin, and thereby forced to cover their private parts as punishment, is something that has never been entirely clear.

"Holy smokes, look at that!"

"Stand back, Eve, we don't know how big this is going to get."

• • •

What *is* crystal clear, however, is that the Japanese have never heard *one word* of this remarkable story—yet they somehow managed to get by for centuries and centuries in blind, unholy ignorance. (I know, it *is* mind-boggling.) They *don't even know* that there's an inherent element of shame connected with sex, nakedness, and all those other awful things (except and unless sanctioned by etc., etc.). If left to their own devices, they'd buy Madonna videos for the music.

Think of all the reinforcement Westerners have benefited from:

1. Stories about Sodom and Gomorrah, plus Lot's wife turning into a pillar of salt. (*That* I would like to have seen. And by the way, what happens when one is "gomorrahized"?)

2. Prostitutes, vilified by one and all (except, one presumes, their customers) and run out of town for having the audacity to try and wash feet for salvation.
3. Salome, employing each and every one of her seven veils, convincing Herod to fetch John the Baptist's head.
4. Archangels assigned to the task of "doing It" instead of good, humble workingmen and husbands.
5. Scarlet letters affixed permanently (so as to warn others away).

Think of the debates in public forum ("We'll hold her head under water, and if she drowns that's proof of her impurity"), concerns for public morality ("You can show them together in bed on the screen, but one foot must be on the floor"), attempts to establish community standards ("What do you mean 'if it goes in' it's obscene? We don't want them in the same room together."). There's a lot to take into account in the West. One hopes one gets it right.

Just in the area of "community standards" alone, AMERI-THINK considers one, all, some, or none of the following:

A. All forms of expression are protected by the First Amendment.
B. That trash is not protected.
C. It's art, therefore it's expression (and therefore it's protected).
D. *Penthouse* may be legal in New York, but it ain't being sold here.
E. If it arouses prurient interests, it's evil.
F. What are prurient interests? The Greek lady in the statue in front of the town library is nekked.
G. So is the guy next to her.

H. Those aren't Greeks, that's Adam and Eve. Before.
I. Breathing heavy—we know what they're doing—is immoral, at least for my children.
J. We don't care about anyone else, you're not buying those records in our town.
K. Parental guidance
L. Under eighteen
M. At least not on prime time
N. Violence is just as immoral.
O. What do you mean, "just as immoral"? That's make-believe killing. Naked is real.
P. What do you mean, "just as immoral"? I'd rather have my kid watch that than senseless butchery.
Q. James Joyce's *Ulysses*
R. That proves my point: James Joyce's *Ulysses*.
S. We're wholesome.
T. We're sophisticated.
U. We're God-fearing.
V. Causes a breakdown of society
W. Is the result of a breakdown of society
X. I don't care what the law says. I have my rights.
Y. Because of rock and roll
Z. Michelangelo

JAPAN-THINK hasn't been able to pull all the above together. They have less experience with our wisdom of the ages and instead revert to what they, at least for the time being, know best. In Japan, Japan is the community. Therefore, one law applies to everyone everywhere. And debate is avoided by making the law very clear. With typical pragmatism, Japanese have come up with simplicity itself.

A. No pubic hair.
   When a clever renegade hit upon the idea of em-
   ploying razors, the law was amended.
B. And no organs—of either kind.

Early visitors from the West landing in Japan all eventually
got around to mentioning in their logs and diaries something
to the effect that the natives seemed to be a jolly, good-
natured lot, but the common folk had the distressing tendency
to walk around "half naked." (Some came right out with it
and said "bare-breasted.")

The early diarists were Spanish and Portuguese missionaries (who could at least read and write), and reference was
made to their attempts to convince the common folk to be
"less shameless" in sartorial matters. (It must be terrible to
be without shame.)

In the late eighteenth and early nineteenth centuries
Dutch traders were allowed limited access to several ports in
Japan, and the reaction of sailors long at sea to the shameless
situation prompted one of the Tokugawa shoguns to issue an
edict to Japanese port workers to keep the womenfolk out
of sight of the barbarians. (An interesting Japanese painting
from that era—in the form and style of today's comic books—
shows several port workers clowning around with long,
pantaloon-type garments in obvious imitation of the barbarian
visitors. Those port workers normally wore little more than
loincloths wrapped around their mid-sections and between
their legs.)

By the time Commodore Perry's black ships arrived, Jiro's
wife and her lady friends wore shirtlike affairs and slightly
bulkier (or fuller) wrappings around their waists and between
their legs when walking around the village. (Actually the
wrappings were really skirts that were pulled up between their
legs by the extension of broad, cloth belts. This is probably

not explained very well, but there you go.) The point is, while working in fields or doing other heavy work during the course of the day, women were still topless. At festival times, and for important village occasions, the common folk (some 95 percent of the population) did wear homespun kimonos in imitation of the upper classes, but shamelessness was still a daily affair.

Not only that, at the end of a long day in the fields one gets hot and sweaty. Communal bathing was the only alternative—not only were private bath facilities in homes extremely rare, doing something like bathing and relaxing all alone was . . . antisocial. But before everyone tries to visualize similar circumstances in Greenwich, Connecticut, remember that Japanese villagers were really in extended family situations—uncles, aunts, grandchildren, in-laws, cousins—in one way or another almost everyone was related through ancestry or marriage. What could be more natural, under those circumstances, than washing off the cares of the day surrounded by friends and relatives—the women keeping an eye on the kids at one end while the men smoked and gossiped at the other—and making plans for the next day or settling arguments (or doing whatever villagers do)? The problem, of course, is that these people hadn't heard about Adam, Eve, and the snake.

Mixed communal bathing extended well into the twentieth century, although prosperity more than a sense of "shame" or sexual decorum led to more segregation by gender—for other reasons men tended to want to be by themselves (and away from the children). The influx of Americans during the Occupation virtually wiped out mixed bathing in cities and resort hotels (Americans knew about the Garden of Eden fiasco), and forced bathhouse proprietors to build a "GI wall" from ceiling to water level in their facilities. Now, one must be pretty far off the beaten path to run across mixed facilities, although many villages in the countryside still have them. (Your author, minding his own business and walking along with his hands in his pockets, once found himself two years ago in a mixed-bathing situation. He, and several hundred of his employees, happened upon a natural hot springs area in the mountains. With the sky for a ceiling and pine trees for walls, he sat immersed to his neck in steamy water while co-workers gamboled like beavers on rocks and logs. Nature and innocence notwithstanding, he still thinks about the girls in the accounting department during long winter evenings—a secret pleasure, if the theory holds, unappreciated by his colleagues that day. Ah, the shame of it all.)

All this is not to say that women stroll along the Ginza today topless. As a matter of fact, Japanese women are becoming known as being perhaps the most fashionably dressed people on earth. The styles may not be as radical as those on the fashion show runway, but they are up-to-date, well-accessoried, and classically tailored. Public demeanor dictates personal conservatism and modesty in dress, knees kept carefully together, and neckline positioning to prevent any glimpse of cleavage.

Yet, and this is the first of many apparent anomalies in this area, displays of nudity in public abound. Several years ago, one of the finest department stores in the country saw fit to hang a banner down the nine-story central gallery of the building as part of a Christmas-decoration scheme. Shoppers—office workers, tourists, children, grandmothers, dirty old men—had nine floors of escalator time to contemplate the banner's caption (Buy Me Now the Christmas I Love) uttered, presumably, by the nine-story beautiful young lady . . . wearing only Santa's hat.

And picture this: a prime-time television program (more about television later) has a feature every few weeks where one of the show's hosts will go out on the street with a cameraman. They visit areas of the city (in the daytime) where girls and young women are likely to be—around universities and department and food stores. They con these girls, fashionably and modestly attired, into showing their breasts "for the fun of it." (At least half the women refuse to do it, but the ones who agree—they are taken to a room in the TV studio—do so while undressing and objecting that their breasts either aren't big or aren't interesting enough. This is videotaped, and the "stars" of this little segment sit with the hosts and panelists on the show at night giggling, blushing, and keeping their knees together.)

AMERI-THINK accepts the braless look and a variety of fashion styles which reveal, among other things, cleavage and legs galore. But a nine-story nude up the side of Saks Fifth Avenue? Probably not.

JAPAN-THINK knows that chaste young ladies should dress like chaste young ladies (bras *and* full slips), but if the occasion arises, showing one's teats on prime-time TV is just one of those things.

(An interesting JAPAN-THINK /AMERI-THINK attitudinal difference arose when Japan's sumo wrestlers made their first appearance in America. These guys, mounds of muscle and beef the size of Herefords, wear only a belt wrapped around their waists and between their legs. Their hindquarters, thus exposed, give them from the rear the appearance of rhinoceri in retreat. AMERI-THINK demanded that they be decently attired during their exhibition bouts. The swim trunks they wore under their belts looked as bizarre to the Japanese as bikini bottoms on Wayne Gretsky would to Americans.)

The acceptance of nakedness in Japan is partially just that—"acceptance." It is a reflection of the general concept that *by itself* nudity is the natural condition, and is something everyone must . . . well, accept. It does cause some confusion to Americans at first. On one hand, there is all to behold in public (mammarian closeups on prime time), yet on the other hand, housewives sit busily at their part-time jobs painting out pubic hair (remember the law) on each and every copy of the relatively innocuous *Playboy* magazines imported from America.

But the acceptance of nakedness leads to a deeper, more complicated issue involving the role of women in society, which in turn leads to all kinds of things including illicit sex and pornography. One plunges into deep water attempting an analysis of this subject, but the whole issue is as representative of Japanese attitudes on "standards of behavior" as a reading of the Bible and a review of *Robert's Rules of Order* reveals an American's "morals" and codes of conduct.

There have been "tradeoffs" between Japanese men and women from time immemorial. When Commodore Perry arrived, Jiro and his ancestors had been measuring their status for centuries by where they stood in the ranks of "workers" or "producers." Although rice cultivation, for example, required the cooperative effort of men and women in the village, clear and different roles evolved. Men did the heaviest of the heavy work and were responsible for conducting events at festival times—women took care of the family home and reared the children. There is nothing particularly unique about this arrangement—other than perhaps more pressure on the men to conform to group ideals—but keep in mind that daily life was conducted without the underlying "religious" attitudes and beliefs common to the West.

Men and women went their ways and did their things. What was "fornication" to the West, with all its moral implications, was merely sexual intercourse to the Japanese. If the man was diligent about maintaining his status in the work effort, and thereafter provided the economic wherewithal for a stable family life, what he did otherwise—drink too much at festival time, dance like a fool in the streets, or get laid a lot—were prerogatives not too dissimilar in consequence.

Authorities on high were not concerned about the issue; the only concern was labor productivity. The titled classes considered it normal for "men of substance" to keep a bevy of mistresses, and a recent TV program in Japan detailed the domestic arrangements in early shogunates in which any and all women employed in the household were "fair game" for nocturnal adventures. (Women were apparently "honored" to be selected for such duty—any children born of the liaisons were well fed and exposed to education while the mothers were made permanent members of the staff.) One shogun was said to have sired nearly one hundred offspring while working his way through a household numbering six hundred ladies-in-waiting. It is more than likely that some (or even many) of the women in those circumstances were unenthusiastic participants in the custom—they must have had boyfriends or lovers back in the villages—but becoming part of a royal household was infinitely better than a lifetime of sloshing about in the mud. "Tradeoffs" were made since there is no evidence these women were captured and held against their wishes.

Obviously traditional behavior is not directly translated to activities today; however, the tendency to accept the "tradeoffs" is. Men are still expected to slave like dogs at the workplace, and women are expected to maintain the home, and rear and educate the children. In public, men are deferred to by women (men are allowed off elevators first, they are served first in restaurants, and wives still walk along at least figuratively one step behind their husbands), and seem to the world at large to be Lords and Masters. It is in fact one of the first things Americans notice about society in Japan—the men have it made and the women are second-class citizens.

The "tradeoff," however, is at home. While ritualized courtesies are made in public—maintaining "face" is important in the group—the man is little more than a vassal in private. Women hold the purse strings, and in an estimated 90 percent of families they control most of the disposable income. The enormity of this came to everyone's attention with the advent of electronic banking in the mid-seventies. Instead of handing out paychecks, money could be transferred to a bank of the employees' choice. Large companies now report that is extremely rare for money to be transferred to an employee account near the workplace. The money all goes to bank branches near the homes. (One organization in Tokyo, the American Club, for some reason continued paying its three hundred employees in cash each month. Efforts to convert to the bank transfer system were objected to by the men, who realized that would create a "paper trail" of *real* earnings—the amount of which they had not gotten around to telling their wives. "Otherwise, we'll be like salarymen living on allowances from our wives.") Despite all the face-saving choreography, it is now common for wives to make all purchases and pay for all meals when families go out on weekends. ("Real men don't handle cash" is the new rationale making the rounds.) There is even the possibility of a case being made that since women in Japan have almost absolute control of domestic money and education, the people are living in a virtually matriarchal society.

For the men, their end of the "tradeoff" is not only being allowed to maintain "face," it's also being allowed to behave in the outside or business world with a minimum of interference from home.

AMERI-THINK housewife to husband leaving for the office: "Be good."

JAPAN-THINK housewife to husband leaving for the office: "Don't let me find out about it."

What is one man's meat is another man's pornography, or even "illicit" sex. As a Japanese man goes about his day, the lure of sexual satisfaction surrounds him. Magazines, including those published by the stuffy National Railway Company for tired, dusty travelers, devote space to photographs of alluring young things in various states of undress. Sports magazines, reporting baseball scores and sumo results, have some of the most spectacular photographs of flesh. Even adult comic books contain illustrated stories of incredible sexual passion and gratification. (Interestingly, mindful of the "no pubic hair, and no organs of either kind" law, the comic book drawings have little blank places where the aforementioned bits occur. Anyone with a little imagination and a ball-point pen could, one supposes, round things out rather nicely.)

Coupled with the printed sexual blitz—magazines of this sort are available on the street in vending machines, by the way—there is also the lure of the "real thing" in countless "live sex shows" and "massage" parlors throughout the land. Dinner with a valued client takes on a mellow glow if preceded by a "total body massage" administered by a lovely young thing wearing bubbles and oil. (Recently, under pressure from the Turkish community in Japan, the government set about correcting a situation, causing some people considerable embarrassment. Because certain establishments were called "Turkish baths"—or "Turkos" in the vernacular—and these establishments offered a range of services up to and including sexual intercourse, an edict came out from "on high." Did the government ban sexual activities in these establishments? No siree. Instead the government decreed that the establishments be henceforth called "soap lands"!)

The official view is that prostitution is neither condoned

nor condemned. As long as the activities are cloaked in something else (i.e., "massage," for example), "prostitution" in the Western sense doesn't really exist. In theory, one could run an operation out of a tea house—several hundred dollars for a cup of tea and beaded curtains.

It is not uncommon for Japanese men to openly (that is, outside the house) brag about a "second wife." It was not that many years ago that the very wealthy built lavish homes for mistresses, according them a status only a step below that of a wife. Today "second wives" are girlfriends or bar hostesses who are "supported" in the sense that expense account money is spent on them or in their business establishments. A man with private assets or excess cash on his hands might "set up" a mistress in her own business—operating a small fashion boutique, tea house (speaking of the devil), or snack bar. The "second wife" grants sexual favors, pampers the man, and otherwise tickles his fancy in a relationship that both know will probably not go beyond that stage and into divorce and remarriage. The "real" wife is the anchor, and raises the kids.

> AMERI-THINK: "Illicit sex and pornography—especially in so public a fashion—is degrading to women, a bad influence on the young, and (probably) immoral."
> JAPAN-THINK: "Er, what?"

Letters to the English-language newspapers in Japan, invariably complaining about the insensitivity of men reading "girly" magazines and adult comic books on the subway during rush hour, are invariably written by non-Japanese women—most of them Americans. Japanese women, no matter what their private thoughts are on the matter, wouldn't dream of doing that. "Being consumed" by sexual matters, to the Japanese, is something that might be considered degrading to both sexes, not just women. But condemnation is limited to that one might expect of drinking too much or wearing an undershirt to dinner with the in-laws. Considering the "trade-offs," it's a nonissue.

The Ministry of Education recently floated a new ruling (which involves obtaining approval from three or four other ministries with a voice in the matter first) suggesting that vending machines selling "girly" magazines be banned within two hundred meters of grade and high schools. The action was applauded in the non-Japanese sector. The *reason* given for this radical move is more interesting than the move itself. Nothing was said about issues affecting the Japanese internally. Instead, the move was prompted by an attempt to "demonstrate to the world we Japanese are international."

Are women in Japan degraded by these things? Degradation, as someone must have said, is in the eye of the beholder. Japanese women have carved out a niche for themselves. While very, very few of them hold any positions of authority or responsibility in major corporations—a yardstick for measuring success in America—they are nevertheless a force to be reckoned with. (Recent interviews with Japanese captains of industry in English-language publications always ask the question: "Can women ever become presidents or managers of your company?" The answers are all variations of the same theme: "Not in my lifetime," "Over my dead body," or "When the sun stops rising in the east.") But Japanese women control family wealth and, even more remarkably, are listed as being the owners or directors of twice as many small businesses (tea shops, fashion boutiques, bars, restaurants, advertising agencies, service companies) as their American female cousins. (And they total only half the Americans in number.) Anyone wishing to debate that the rigors and challenges of dealing with napkin suppliers, liquor wholesalers, company unions, dress manufacturers, landlords, language teachers, delivery services, and head-on customers are any easier than being a vice-president of Citibank will have a fight on his or her hands.

What is more important, society in Japan is geared to supporting the "company effort" of men working in whatever is considered to be the industry of the moment. The pressures of home and family are relatively unimportant and less distracting than the single-minded dedication one must devote to "the company." Provided the home fires are regularly fueled, the paycheck is there, and "abuses" in the Western sense are kept outside the family circle, anything goes.

As one gentleman explained, when caught red-handed in an *affaire de coeur,* "it was on my way home." It went a long way toward alleviating the consequences of behavior "outside the parameters of decency" in Japan.

AMERI-THINK: "I don't buy that."
JAPAN-THINK: "He was at least home before midnight."

13

· · ·

KEEPING UP WITH THE
WATANABES

AMERI-THINK: "All things being equal, conspicuous consumption has a lot going for it."
JAPAN-THINK: "Well, I suppose . . . by that I mean to say, ah, consumption is . . . er, well, of course, it is . . . something we all . . . more or less . . . do—but that's not to say that we, I mean *it,* should be, ah, conspicuous. Yes, of course not."

The perceptive reader may notice a subtle ambivalence in the second statement. The Japanese, who are on target toward becoming the Grand Consumer Champions Of All Time, are still a little uncomfortable about it all.

The only people roaming the streets of Japan born and raised in a stable country with relative wealth are in their early teens or younger. All adults—even those born in the 1960s—endured some amount of "hard times" in the journey to today.

Those born before, during, or immediately after the war, of course, were raised in families where starvation was a real possibility, new or used clothing of any kind was treasured, patched, and repatched, and "the luxury of space" meant a place to sleep on the floor (indoors).

Now and then one will run across an older Japanese still wearing a Hamilton wristwatch or carrying a Parker fountain pen. Although the well-to-do always had luxury items, they were a relatively small group in the overall mass of people. "I was the first in my school to have one," or "Nobody in my family had ever even *seen* one" will be the proud remark.

Consumption has long meant purchasing mere necessities in Japan. Not only did this fit the Japanese temperament— simplicity is best—it also reflected the times. Very few people had money. Even the decor and architecture of traditional Japanese houses discouraged the introduction of large (and expensive) Western furniture like dining room sets, couch and chair combinations, and related bric-a-brac. Scraping together enough money to purchase a used set of golf clubs probably represented the first nonessential purchase in Japan after the war. (One hesitates purchasing a yacht when (a) there's no car to pull it, (b) no docks for launching it, and (c) it's bigger than the house.)

Compare those circumstances to the "life-style" of an average American born during the war. (Your author's brother—whom he dearly loves and secretly envies—has been selected as an "example" of the startling highs one can achieve in the art of consumerism on a normal salary.)

AMERI-POSSESSIONS:

A. One wife
B. Two children

C. One very large dog (who jumps into bed with visiting relatives)
D. One house in the suburbs
E. One cabin at the lake
F. One shiny, black car (for self)
G. One less shiny clunker (for wife)
H. One Corvette (which goes like hell during the eight or nine times per year it's let out of the garage)
I. One motorcycle (for the times there's the need for bugs on the forehead and teeth)
J. A jet boat (which can go in the ocean or run in two inches of water)
K. A sit-down, drive-it-around lawn mower (with an engine larger than the one in your author's car)
L. A houseful of furniture that is all coordinated and/or matches
M. A rec room in the basement containing a bar, toilet, television sets, recorders, an exercise room, an ice hockey rink, part of a football field, and God only knows what else (just kidding about the last two things)

Taking the average Japanese salaryman with the same income relative to his station in Japan, and plopping him down in the midst of all this, could seriously damage his nervous system. He'd think he had died and gone to heaven.

But the Japanese are working on it. It's just that the restrictions of space and the cost of land give a twist to the nature of consumption.

· Everyone's Doing It ·

Probably nowhere on earth is the "everyone's doing it" rationale (or excuse) more important than it is in Japan. During the "hard times"—and that is up until ten or fifteen years ago—the well-to-do downplayed their good fortune and spent money either on fine arts (which could be kept discreetly at home) or on lavish *overseas* vacation retreats in places like Hawaii and the South Pacific islands. Since everyone was *not* "doing it," i.e., displaying wealth conspicuously, no one "did it."

Once the average man began to accumulate significant savings, coupled with the increasing strength of the yen against all currencies including the American dollar, a few timid stabs at consuming conspicuously were made. Families began purchasing automobiles in greater numbers. In 1980, for example, 62 percent of all cars sold in Japan were sold to people *who had never owned* a car before. (One fallout of the trade issue involving Japanese exports to America and the "voluntary" restrictions on the numbers of cars exported is the very real fear that the day will come—as the Japanese auto manufacturers redirect their efforts in the domestic market—when the length of all autos end-to-end in Japan exceeds the length of all roads, streets, and highways. In fact, it may happen next Friday.)

Next, the strong yen allowed Japanese to begin purchasing foreign luxury automobiles. Until recent years only gangsters and politicians (it's a coincidence, folks, mere coincidence) drove Lincoln Continentals or Mercedes-Benzes. Now, owning a BMW, Jaguar, or a Porsche is "in," and sales are increasing each year. The buyer profile is probably not much different than that for Americans in the States. (An interesting turnabout is exemplified by the fact that Americans working for American companies in Japan drive beat-up Hondas.) A mint-condition, early-model Corvette, for example (now driven only eight or nine times a year when it's allowed out of the garage), would fetch a small fortune in Japan.

In the world of fashion, bringing back expensive "name" handbags from duty-free shops in Hawaii was "okay" as it was less a question of flaunting wealth than it was a realization that the items were by Japanese standards "dirt-cheap." They then became symbols of overseas trips, and now, with cheaper imitations made in Hong Kong and Taiwan, they are part of the standard uniform of every female over the age of twelve in Japan.

Designer dresses have now become *de rigueur*. A soirée of a hundred or so people in Tokyo could involve a half million dollars of cut and trimmed cloth. Gold chains, diamonds, and Rolex watches are extra. Suddenly, everyone *is* doing it, because . . . everyone is doing it. With a vengeance.

Gourmet dinners and entertainment at major hotels and clubs can run five hundred dollars a head—and there are waiting lists. (And there are waiting lists for yachts purchased but undelivered while docking facilities are being constructed.) Packaged trips "off the beaten paths" abroad (i.e., not Hawaii) are available for families with nice little extras like accompanying babysitters and doctors. Plunking down several thousand dollars a head for a long weekend is "just the thing" to soothe the nerves.

A revealing experience has been driving past the same private nursery school/kindergarten every morning for ten years. Originally the mothers showed up with their children in the type of housedresses one would expect mothers to show up in at eight o'clock in the morning. (It can't be any easier getting a Japanese kid to finish his fish entrails than it is getting an American kid to finish his oatmeal.) The last few years have been a revelation, however. Now the mothers show up dressed to the nines—fur coats, exquisite coiffures, and chains and bangles worth a king's ransom. Not only that, if the mothers can't pull it all together in time, a private limousine service is available to usher the little toddlers to their modeling blocks and clay. (It used to be that most mothers and kids arrived at the school on bicycles—the mother pedaling with the child hanging on at the rear. This year only one mother does that, and she hides the bicycle in bushes around the corner from the school.)

Parents and grandparents have a lot more money to spend, and indulging children is a way of keeping up with the Watanabes, if not going slightly ahead. Besides, with fewer children per family, the indulgence can be more sharply focused. An Associated Press story in the *Japan Times* recently reported on a department store advertising campaign featuring models in pearl chokers, designer gowns, lace gloves, and for the males a double-breasted tux and top hat. The ensembles could be had for a measly $3,000. The models were preschoolers. The young mothers, growing up reading magazines about fashions that were unattainable at the time, are going around the bend in conspicuous consumerism for their children.

Is anybody worried about this? Not so much when it's adults spending money on themselves. They have worked hard for prosperity, and their pleasures are really no different than my brother's boat.

But Japan is raising a generation of children whose experiences and expectations in life will be radically different from those of their parents. Obtaining *now* what one wants *now*—without the necessity of working and waiting—is a brand-new phenomenon in Japan.

One thing is certain: it would knock Jiro and his wife for a loop.

Chapter

14

. . .

SERVICE, ANYONE?

Say what you will about America's "Service While U Wait," "One-Stop Fast Service," or "Service with a Smile" campaigns, there is no place on earth where service is as *consistently* good as it is in Japan.

The key may be consistency. Every shop, store, and restaurant—from the largest and most glamorous emporium to the hole-in-the-wall factory outlet—greets visitors as if they are long-lost relatives returning from exile. (Some have argued that the "greetings" and "good-byes" all shopkeepers utter on all occasions are merely programmed sounds and don't reflect conscious thought. That could be—but what a nice thing to program.)

The quality and elegance of "service" in Japan are probably the result of two things. Given the right circumstances, Japanese people genuinely want to be nice. And, perhaps as important, Japanese shoppers are the fussiest in creation. The shopper/shoppee relationship is frequently the only reason people give for putting up with the noise, crowds, hustle and bustle of city living in Japan.

AMERI-THINK considers service "good" when the restaurant after a fashion brings more or less what was ordered. (And don't be misled by "Chuck," who introduces himself and reels off the dozen specials not appearing on the menu. One seldom sees "Chuck" again after his opening performance.)

JAPAN-THINK considers service "good" when the restaurant provides both hot *and* cold towels for the hungry patron, all the staff including the dishwashers and chef visit the table, a choice of everything on the menu is provided *plus* anything available in the Eastern Hemisphere (which the chef will go out, buy, and cook), the appetizers are presented attractively (in the color and shape of wild flowers, cute animals, or butterfly wings), the main course is served with an exotic sauce made of ingredients no one's ever heard of (but which the waiter, busboy, and cashier will try to describe— although none of them can "think of the right words" for it), the dessert is served in either flames or on dry ice, and the check is delivered by the maître d', who has crawled across the floor to the table on his belly. (JAPAN-THINK would consider the service excellent if the chef pulled up a chair and joined the meal.) Anything less than the above, and the restaurant wouldn't have customers within a month.

It is thought that human interaction between buyer and seller is important in Japan. For several reasons, not the least of which is that old bugaboo "space," self-service shopping is less popular in Japan than in America. There just isn't room to spread out all merchandise on miles of shelves. An American can purchase most necessities of life without interacting with anyone but a cashier. Not so the Japanese. The purchase of most things involves selection and decision in conversation with someone. During the ritual conversation, the seller assumes subtle responsibility for his products, the buyer accepts the responsibility of being a good and steady customer. It is comforting to both sides. (The self-service stores that *do* exist in Japan are primarily in the prepackaged, convenience-store category. Not much conversation is required for purchasing canned beans or toilet paper.) The role-playing on the sides of the buyer and seller confirms the importance of "service" in any transaction, and that concept has become a golden thread in the tapestry of life in Japan.

Consider this: Japanese garbage collectors recently picked up a paper shopping bag containing dirty dress shirts destined for the laundry. (An American businessman in Tokyo "mixed up" laundry day and garbage day—but that's another story.) The bag of shirts was thrown into the gaping jaws of the garbage truck, swallowed, and carted off to the waste disposal plant at the edge of Tokyo Bay. There, the bag was disgorged onto a pile of garbage from the homes of some twelve million people in the neighborhood.

Brave workmen with hip boots and long rakes sort the stuff into various piles depending upon incineration category. (The landfill project is ambitious in Japan. By sometime next century, people will be able to walk from Tokyo to Honolulu.) One of the brave workmen happened upon the bag of shirts. Looking at them, he decided a mistake had been made. He took them to his supervisor.

The fact that the American businessman got his shirts back is not the point of this story. (The garbage people saw a non-Japanese name printed on the inside of the collars and contacted the seven laundry associations in Tokyo and Yokohama. They sent out fliers to the member laundries in each of their groups, and sure enough one laundry had a customer by that name. Since the American businessman was never home during laundry working hours, and the laundry had no way of getting in touch with him, they contacted the janitor

at his apartment building. *He* had no
worked, but he had noticed that hi
parking sticker on the windshiel
contacted, and then in turn the A
"Sure enough," it was reported, "my

No, the point is not that the shirts were
just another only-in-Japan example of organizatio.
questioned by foreign reporters about the shirt episode, th
garbage folks explained that they always keep an eye out for
things that might be thrown away by mistake. "False teeth
and urns of cremated ashes sometimes turn up," it was explained.) The point is the general subject of "service" and the
condition of the shirts upon their return. After all they went
through, smothered in yakitori orts and fish heads, the shirts
were returned freshly laundered. And someone along the
way, who knows where, had neatly sewed a button—which
had been missing for months—on the sleeve of one of the
shirts.

· Quality of Goods ·

AMERI-QUIZ: "Who is W. E. Deming? Uh . . . a
football player?"
JAPAN-QUIZ: "Who is W. E. Deming? Are you kidding me? He's the most famous American—next to
General MacArthur and Pete Rose."

Dr. Deming arrived in Japan after the war. His expertise
lay in the area of quality control. He introduced the concept
of establishing in manufacturing plants a "quality circle" of a
half dozen employees who in addition to their regular jobs
would meet for an hour or so every couple weeks to review
quality control and study productivity improvement tech-

His theory was that Japan would do better for itself image of manufacturing cheap and shoddy products was and instead Japan develop the image (and reality) of gh-quality goods and merchandise. By the early 1960s most firms had quality-control circles, many plants were working on "zero defect" targets, "Made in Japan" no longer meant crap products, and Dr. Deming was on his way to being elevated to a plateau in Japan approaching godhood. To this day, engineering clubs are named after him, and it is not unusual for Japanese business pilgrims to visit him on trips to America. (The fact that his work is relatively unknown in America is a continuing puzzle to his former disciples in Japan, but the irony is noted when Americans visit Japan to study quality-control techniques.)

Dr. Deming's achievements notwithstanding, making products very carefully is natural in a society not too far removed from preindustrial days when craftsmen made things by hand, and succeeded or failed on how skillfully they went about their tasks. Too many lacquered soup bowls that leak, and one is back hauling sacks of rice for a living. And combining this appreciation of fine craftsmanship with the commitment to provide quality service makes shopping in Japan a pleasant experience. (But the consumer is still fussy.)

AMERI-THINK: "The hem on this dress is not completely sewn. Is there a discount?"
JAPAN-THINK: "The hem on this dress is not completely sewn. It should be thrown away."

One problem in Japan is the tendency to institutionalize things. This is fine in many areas, but it contributes to curious blind spots in the service sector. If, for example, the training manual says "All items purchased in this store must be nicely and carefully wrapped," the sales clerks will therefore "nicely

and carefully" wrap everything put before them—from dia-
mond necklaces to flashlight batteries—even though the line
at the counter is two blocks long. (Significant portions of a
novel can be read waiting in line in bookstores while clerks
not only wrap packages of books but also cover and wrap
each book individually.)

Institutionalization destroys flexibility, and that is happening in a Japan that is more comfortable programming results and then working like hell to get them rather than leaving
matters up to individual judgment. Observe the following
service scenarios.

AMERICA

CUSTOMER: "Salad, ham and cheese sandwich, cof-
fee."
WAITRESS: "Yeah, Mac. French, Italian, bleu
cheese, oil and vinegar, or creamy yogurt?"
CUSTOMER: "What?"
WAITRESS: "On your salad. Whaddya think I
meant?"
CUSTOMER: "Oh, ah, oil and vinegar."
WAITRESS: "White, whole wheat, rye, cracked bar-
ley, or oat?"
CUSTOMER: "What . . . oh, I know. White."
WAITRESS: "Swiss, American, or goat?"
CUSTOMER: "No, ham."
WAITRESS: "Look, Bud, I know ham. I'm talking
cheese."
CUSTOMER: "It really doesn't . . . er, American."
WAITRESS: "Decaf or regular?"
CUSTOMER: "You're talking coffee, right?"
WAITRESS: "Hey, pal, I ain't got all day."
CUSTOMER: "Regular."

CUSTOMER: "This is rye bread. I ordered white."

WAITRESS: "Tough. We're outta white. Have a nice day."

JAPAN

WAITRESS: "Welcome to our humble establishment. Are we ever glad to see you here. Sit by the window if it pleases you. You can see better to eat, read, or generally goof off while you're spending your precious time with us."

CUSTOMER: "Perfect. I've been out shopping all morning and my feet are killing me."

WAITRESS: "Here, take off your shoes and we'll get someone to rub your feet."

CUSTOMER: "No, that's all right. Just a little lunch will do."

WAITRESS: "What a good idea, this being a restaurant and all. I guess we're both lucky."

CUSTOMER: "I'll have salad, ham and cheese sandwich, and coffee."

WAITRESS: "Oh, I'm so sorry. I feel as bad about this as you can imagine. I could kill myself. A thousand pardons, but salad comes with other things. The *sandwich set* comes with soup."

CUSTOMER: "Oh, that's quite all right. I've had too much salad lately anyway. Don't feel bad about it. What kind of soup is it?"

WAITRESS: "Today's. You'll like it."

CUSTOMER: "Oh, that sounds good."

WAITRESS: "One more thing. I'm so embarrassed I could die. I may crawl under the table with shame. Ham and cheese sandwiches aren't on our humble menu. We have either ham sandwiches or cheese sandwiches, but not ham and cheese sandwiches."

CUSTOMER: "That makes perfectly good sense. I apologize for being so inconsiderate and not studying the menu with care and concern. Kindly make it ham."

WAITRESS: "A brilliant decision. I knew you'd make the right choice. I'll bring the tea with your meal."

CUSTOMER: "Coffee."

WAITRESS: "We don't serve coffee until after lunch hour. It's just one of those things."

CUSTOMER: "The meal was so exquisitely prepared it was almost a pity to eat it."

WAITRESS: "It was our pleasure. The chef and his entire family will be glad to hear that. And come back again and try our curry rice set. It comes with salad."

Japanese want to "get it right," and if this means paring down individual choices to a streamlined few, that's what will happen. The bank clerks who hand out only new currency, the ones who wrap individual strawberries or oranges in packages that are themselves works of art, the polite and attentive waiters and waitresses, and the cashiers who chase customers through crowded streets, up and down stairs, and around corners to return ten-cent overcharges are all part of the charm of Japan.

But ask one of them to do something outside the "job description," and it will take several meetings at all levels to work out the details. The coffee may be spilled in your lap in America, but at least it's coffee.

Chapter

15

. . .

POP CULTURE, TELEVISION,
AND THE BLITZ OF MEDIA

· Pop Culture ·

Remember, back in the good old days, when one kid would show up on the playground with a yo-yo? (For those born in the electronic game era, a yo-yo was a round plastic or wood thing with a string attached, and by clever manipulation the plastic or wood thing could be made to go up and down on the string. Oh, boy. Up and down. Up and down. Up and down. Young computer whizzes today don't know what they're missing. Up and down. Up and down. Wow.) Within a week, every kid in the school had a yo-yo (up and down), and within a month or two, every kid in America had a yo-yo (UP AND DOWN).

The same could be said of marbles, Frisbees, Hula-Hoops and even Pet Rocks. The item would be introduced, spread like wildfire on a local basis within weeks, and by the end of the summer the nation would succumb to the craze. Within a year of their introduction, Barbie (and Ken) Dolls were being cuddled, pampered and dressed from Maine to California—in households of every religious, economic, and racial persuasion.

Now then, picture Japan. There are four national commercial television stations, three national noncommercial stations, and several regional commercial stations. There are four or five radio stations. There are a half-dozen national newspapers, and perhaps as many regional papers. (The newspapers also own four of the television stations.) The most popular weekly news magazine is "seen" by an estimated 30 percent of the population. An interesting idea is mentioned in passing on the 7:00 P.M. news, and by noon the following day the entire nation knows about it, or is clamoring for it. Fads can develop faster in all of Japan than they do in one individual *family* in America.

Provided the product catches on, Japan is a marketer's dream. Fortunes have been made in stuffed animals, representations of cartoon characters, and of course now all the software for computer games. (Tens of thousands of junior high school boys in different locations all over the country lined up for two days or more in the snow and ice to purchase the latest software for one of the games.) A drama on television a year ago featured a popular high school–aged girl who was having "love problems." She wrote her longed-for boyfriend's name on the back of one hand and covered it with a Band-Aid. The next day there was a run on Band-Aids in Japan—merchants had difficulty keeping them in stock.

Although fads come and go, the Japanese are surprisingly loyal to items or people once adored. In the 1960s, a Little Black Sambo–type doll became very popular—many of the dolls had flexible arms so that they could be attached to bicycle handlebars, school bags, or study lamps. The dolls no longer fall into the "fad" category, but they're still for sale, and mothers who had them before still buy them for their children. When it was pointed out recently by non-Japanese that the dolls might be demeaning to many people by perpetuating stereotypical portrayals, their sale was reluctantly discontinued. But there is still a flourishing underground trade in them.

When it comes to people once adored, a number of Western personalities and show business performers appeared in Japan right at the time television was becoming popular and mass media was fine-tuning its attack. Some of the people came back several times over the years, and they are now treasured in the minds and memories of Japanese at a level just one notch below the acclaim granted to that fabulous superstar of quality control, Dr. W. E. Deming.

1. *Fred MacMurray* ("My Three Sons" was an early television show from America, and the dubbing into Japanese was done so skillfully, folks thought old Fred was fluent. Couldn't get enough of the man.)

2. *Joe DiMaggio* (Not only did he do his graceful thing with the New York Yankees in Japan, he later showed up with the next name on the list.)

3. *Marilyn Monroe* (Photographers treasure their negatives of shots of her getting into the car with Joe and getting out of the car with Joe.)

4. *Alain Delon* (Being a French actor he doesn't belong in this book, but now and then one will meet a pudgy, balding Japanese who claims people used to think he looked like Alain Delon when he was younger.)

5. *Paul Anka* (What could be more remarkable than a nation producing both a singer of his talent and an actress of Marilyn's range?)

6. *James Coburn* ("Our Man Flint" had to be the coolest

creature ever to walk this earth. He still sells cigarettes in Japan.)

7. *Sammy Snead* (Sweetest swing in golf—men are still copying it with umbrellas on subway platforms.)

No list of "famous" Americans in the early- to middle-postwar era would be complete without the name of Douglas MacArthur. He represented the "conquerors," but in contrast to what was feared of him, he turned out to be in Japanese minds a wise and benevolent leader. To say that following his exploits in Japan was a "fad" is not quite right. But the hysteria of swooning bobbysoxers at Frank Sinatra concerts in the 1940s was not unlike the attention paid to MacArthur's son Arthur, who was a teenager during the Occupation.

Of course there are "pop" heroes today in Japan whose stars are more recently risen—Madonna is a big hit, anything to do with the Beatles is newsworthy (John Lennon's widow is Japanese; Paul McCartney was thrown into the slammer for bringing grass to Tokyo), Billy Joel had a concert last week, and it goes on. In fact, most rock groups try to make regular visits to the country. The market is huge, and there's always the chance they'll become cult figures. (But they'll have to go a long way to catch up to Fred MacMurray.)

One interesting fad in Japan has become something approaching a subculture for a fairly broad range of people in Japan. Remember Philco radios, Li'l Abner, Norman Rockwell covers for the *Saturday Evening Post,* tulip-shaped Coca-Cola glasses, Blatz beer signs, jukeboxes, Captain Midnight decoder rings, saddle shoes, Virgil Partch cartoons, 78 rpm records, Ovaltine canisters, cardigan high school letter sweaters, and cap pistols? They're all in Japan, and collectors abound. Youngsters travel for miles each Sunday to dance in Tokyo's parks wearing crinoline skirts. (Their partners all look like the Ames Brothers.) Some Japanese businessmen, on their trips abroad, spend their spare time looking for vacuum tubes for old radios. The Budweiser beer logo, initially popular in Japan from the old metal serving trays, and later as a symbol on T-shirts, finally became popular on . . . beer. (The company went from exporting a few hundred cases a year a decade ago to now being one of the best-selling foreign beers in Japan.) The only explanation anyone can think of for all of this is the fact that the period of history represented by these items was a period of void in Japan. For thirty years, beginning in the mid-thirties, the Japanese were either preparing for, fighting, or recovering from the war.

· Television ·

Entertainment is entertainment, and Japanese approach the phenomenon in much the same way as Americans. Programs come and go, stars are hot and cold, and there are too many commercials. Two notable exceptions exist in Japan, however. There is a government supported, noncommercial entity (much like the BBC in England) which operates two channels. They produce a broad range of informational, educational, and mixed entertainment features that are in most cases superb in execution and content. (All households with television sets pay an annual fee to partially subsidize the operation.) The other exception has to do with the role of advertisers (more about advertising later) vis-à-vis programming on the commercial stations. Although "ratings" of a show are important, there is less of a direct relationship between viewing figures and advertising rates. The powerful Japanese ad agencies buy space and time for all major clients on virtually all stations and shows.

Otherwise, the major categories of programming are the same. But what goes on inside those categories is at times wildly different.

Period Drama

This category in America is (or was) made up primarily of stories of the Wild West—cowboys, Indians, settlers, and Boot Hill. The cycle has run its course for a while, but you get the idea. In Japan the cowboy story becomes the samurai story. Swashbucklers roam the countryside of two hundred years ago, keeping peace, falling in love, fighting the bad guys, yelling at each other, and getting into trouble. No cattle appear in the stories, a lot more pretty girls do, and people go off into the sun*rise* at the end. These types of programs will go on forever in Japan it seems—there are a half dozen at least per week.

Contemporary Drama

American contemporary drama tends to run to serials—nighttime versions of daytime soap operas ("Dallas," "Knots Landing," the late lamented "St. Elsewhere," etc.). With a broad cast of characters, nearly every form of lust, greed, bigamy, and unholy alliance can be worked around the occasional wrongful death and embezzlement scam. The Japanese haven't really gotten around to this yet—their soap operas remain daytime fare. They have prime-time programs with lust, greed, bigamy, and the other good stuff, but each evening's show tends to be a complete story in itself. Popular actors and actresses regularly appear in these programs, and one must pay attention carefully—the cute girl with a slight overbite might be someone's tomboy sister one week and a drooling nymphomaniac the next.

Cops and Robbers

Here things get a little silly. Early American television shows were like Jack Webb's "Dragnet." Joe Friday and his pal

Frank—in spiffy suits and haircuts—would plod around for days investigating armed robberies of mom-and-pop stores (which we'd never actually see), auto thefts (which we'd never actually see), and cats belonging to little old ladies stuck up in trees (which we'd never actually see). Today, these programs have evolved to the point where we have dope addicts, tattooed greaseballs in pimp outfits, sexual deviants, slippery characters in designer shirts, child molesters, and all the flotsam and jetsam of a graffitied underworld engaged in mortal combat for survival. Moreover, it's never clear until the denouement which are the good guys and which are the bad guys. Japan loves this, and has ripped off the style. Although Japanese police in reality would make Joe Friday and Frank look like incorrigible hippies on the extreme fringe of society, the television programs portray "detectives" dressed as zoot-suiters, rock-and-roll idols, high school dropouts, and fashion models with confused hormones cracking down on crime. (To show their commitment to things and disdain of protocol, they *wear shoes* in houses when grilling suspects.) Given the circumstances in Japan, however, the shows take on a surreal, fairy-tale appearance. The detectives are investigating armed robberies of convenience stores (which we never actually see), auto thefts (which we never actually see), and cats belonging to little old ladies stuck up in trees (which we never actually see).

Game Shows

These programs have two basic attractions. "Playing along"— guessing the answers before the contestants—is one attraction. Watching common citizens making fools of themselves over bedroom sets, trips to Jamaica, or a month's salary in cash is another. Although both attractions exist in American shows, there is a tendency to feature the fat lady in a chicken costume guessing which of the three doors hides a fur coat and camping equipment for the entire family. Japan has no shows in the latter category. Everything is geared toward "playing along." Of particular interest are the Japanese game shows—perhaps half of them—which concentrate on the puzzles of things abroad. Film clips of a chirpy young girl interviewing yak herders in Tibet, stone masons in Italy, or dairy farmers in Kansas will create questions about a particular custom or implement employed in the profession. ("Oh, *that's* what they use to impregnate sheep!") On one hand, Japanese look outward, and the game shows provide a format for international exposure and education. On the other hand, those game shows reinforce ethnocentrism ("Look what those crazy foreigners do when they bury their dead.") The jury is still out on this issue.

Variety Shows

American television started with this format. Uncle Miltie, Sid Caesar, the dynamic Ed Sullivan, Jackie Gleason—even Jack Benny, Bing Crosby, Bob Hope, and Perry Como—came up with a mix of comedy, music, skits, and general freewheeling entertainment recorded "live" in front of real people watching the action. "That Was the Week That Was" carried on the tradition, as does "Saturday Night Live" currently. But the format has given way to "comedy sit-coms," canned, rehearsed, and dubbed. Variety shows are alive, well, and flourishing in *Japan*—they not only form the bulk of TV programming, they increase in numbers each year. The problem is that dedicated "Honeymooners" fans will cringe in despair at the level of sophistication in the beloved format. Although some shows appear to play to adult audiences (funny skits about checking into love hotels), most of the programs are directed toward those in junior and senior high school (judging by age levels in the audience). College students dropping their pants, rolling onto their backs, pulling their legs up, and competing with each other in duels of flatulence (for a hysterical audience splitting its sides) would fall a bit below the mark in America. Teenagers running through obstacle courses (with the girls in T-shirts doused in water), cross-dressed boys and girls having pillow fights, and fourteen-year-olds singing Billie Holiday songs ("Cry Me a River," complete with cute choreography) are summer camp high jinks wrought large (or at least wrought national).

Talk Shows

In America these tend to incorporate audiences into the show. Johnny, Oprah, Phil, Joan, Arsenio, *et al.* play to the audiences, ask them questions, and generally interact with them one way or the other. Talk shows in Japan are really *talk* shows—the guest and host are in a one-on-one situation—and the event is taped in a silent studio. The interviews go into greater detail and depth than those in America, but then again one must be prepared to spend an hour listening to a third baseman describe his feelings about striking out in the Japan Series.

Late-Night Shows

In America it's David Letterman and, ah, David Letterman. There are three similar shows in Japan, but instead of focusing on the "star" ("Oh, what crazy guys me and Paul are"), the Japanese host, accompanied by a demure young girl at his side (whose job is to agree with everything the host says), will take the viewer on taped trips of Tokyo night life, behind the scenes of sex film production, into bars and strip joints, and basically to all the places one might visit if possessed of enough money, energy, and intestinal fortitude.

News Programs

In this category, America and Japan have virtually identical formats—and both are excellent. Because most television stations in Japan cover the entire nation, it does take some getting used to when the newscasters suddenly switch from events in the Middle East to the problems confronting Mr. Watanabe and his rice crop.

Both nations also produce excellent documentaries—the Civil War series in America is matched by the Silk Road series in Japan. If anything, the government-supported, people-subsidized noncommercial station in Japan is able to explore subjects a little more off the beaten path, so if the subject is your cup of green tea, it can be a fine evening of televiewing. Included in this category are concerts, operas, jazz performances, visits to museums, live drama, Japanese dance, and ballet.

In the world of sports, the attitudes are as follows:

AMERI-THINK: If a lot is good, more is better.
JAPAN-THINK: If a lot is good, more is better.

The only difference between the two countries is in the area of variety. If "sports widows" (or widowers) in America believe they have a cause, consider what faces their opposites in Japan.

AMERI-JOCK
(regularly scheduled):
    A. Football (professional)
    B. Football (college)
    C. Baseball (professional)
    D. Basketball (professional)

E. Basketball (college)
F. Track and field
G. Golf
H. Hockey (professional)
I. Miscellaneous (horse racing, auto racing, bowling, tennis, and all the things the "sports networks" fill time with)

JAPAN-JOCK
(regularly scheduled):
A. Football (company-sponsored teams)
B. Football (college)
C. Baseball (professional)
D. Baseball (college)
E. Baseball (high school. Japanese stop what they're doing during the twice-a-year *national* tournaments.)
F. Rugby (company-sponsored teams)
G. Rugby (college)
H. Rugby (high school)
I. Sumo (national sport. Every minute of six fifteen-day tournaments is televised, *twice* a day.)
J. Basketball (company-sponsored and college. Men's *and* women's teams get equal coverage.)
K. Volleyball (along with baseball, Japan's unofficial national sport. During the season, i.e., all the time except summer, men's and women's teams of all ilk are "on the air" several times a week.)
L. Judo (another unofficial national sport. Champions are national heroes.)
M. Boxing (Remember the days before closed-circuit bouts? Boxing is regular fare in Japan.)
N. Track and field (same as America, but more programs dipping to the high school level)

O. Marathons (Not only are there televised marathons at least once a weekend, there are *relay* televised marathons at least once a weekend—teams from companies, colleges, high schools, men, women, and mixed running over hill and dale, screwing up traffic from dawn to dusk.)

P. Skiing (Keep in mind that Japan is 80 percent mountainous, and there isn't a man, woman, or child in the nation who hasn't been on the slopes.)

Q. Hockey (Not only are there company-sponsored teams; the college circuit is big-time, and heavily covered.)

R. Auto racing (This is not in the miscellaneous category—the Japanese are now the biggest sponsors of these events in the world.)

S. Motorcycle racing (same as above)

T. Wrestling (Most "stars" from America compete in Japan, international championships are held, and female wrestlers are popular guests on variety shows.)

U. Tennis (Whereas big tournaments are shown in America, those plus "tennis lesson" clips of ten or fifteen minutes each are shown nightly in Japan.)

V. Horse racing (Along with speed-boat racing, horse racing is one of the few events on which gambling is legal.)

W. Golf (Whereas sumo is the official national sport, golf is the official national mania. Not only are the big tournaments shown, almost everything local is shown. There are golf tournaments involving stars from other sports, stars from show business, blind people, people who've never played golf before, cute young "music talents," hospital porters, dwarfs, bar hostesses, and former Japanese soldiers who refused to surrender

and lived in jungles for decades. Added to the above
regular programs include, like tennis, daily lessons in
ten- or fifteen-minute clips.)
X. Miscellaneous (kendo—hitting people with sticks;
karate—hitting things with hands; kick boxing—hitting opponents with feet)
Y. Golf
Z. More golf

Television is said to reflect national consciousness and
attitudes. That may be true, but as said at the outset, entertainment is entertainment. And how novel can a program be,
given the constraints of time and the dimensions of the tube?
The only generalities that can be made are the following two.
The problem is, one tends to reflect national character, the
other is the opposite of the presumed character.

AMERI-TIME: People can set their watches by when the
"Cosby Show" comes on or the "Tonight" show goes off.
With the exception of major sporting events (having learned
from the "*Heidi*" fiasco"), the networks program shows in neat
blocks beginning either on the hour or half hour. Week to
week, the times remain constant.

JAPAN-TIME: In a nation where trains enter and leave
stations *on the second* (not on the minute, on the second),
precision in craftsmanship is treasured, and the standard measure of distance is the millimeter, television programs begin
at times like 8:43 and end at 9:26—more or less. The same
program the following week might start at 8:31 and run all
the way to 9:54. The only exception to this, and this is what
blows the minds of *all* baseball fans, is that the nightly televised games end whenever the schedule for that day says the
games should end. ("Two out, bottom of the ninth, bases
loaded, three runs behind, Hara steps to the plate. Good

night, everybody, and let's humbly thank our sponsors for bringing us this game.")

Something about the above doesn't seem right. Flexibility is an American trait, rigidity is Japanese (and yet they stress it in the only area where the timing of the event is uncontrollable.) The following is probably more indicative of national character.

AMERI-YUKS: Sit-coms have weekly plots with the stars reacting and behaving in accordance with the story line. ("You mean Dick nailed his hand to the barn wall again? Go get Larry and his brothers to help.") The story's the thing, and the predictability of the characters in the plotted situation is the humor of it all.

JAPAN-YUKS: Sit-coms don't exist as such in Japan. (There are programs, for example, where "three zany office ladies" might mistake their boss for the village rapist, and funny little things happen to them as they get to the bottom of it all, but there is no pretense of the show being a playlet performed in front of an audience laughing hysterically. The shows are more like short movies à la *Nine to Five*.) What the Japanese like are real people put in various humorous, awkward, or embarrassing situations. No "story" is involved— the "event" is triggered by a water-filled balloon in the pants, a girlfriend catching a boyfriend "en flagrante," or an accountant going up to bat against a professional ballplayer. The real person—not an obvious "character"—reacts in a predictable fashion. And the giggling, blushing, and genuine embarrassment is reinforcement of what *everybody* would naturally feel in those circumstances, not "characters" in a contrived situation. The *range* of responses in Americans— anger, humor, indifference, and belligerence in shows like "Candid Camera"—is interesting to Americans. The *similarities* of responses are comforting to Japanese.

A final note on television (and newspapers as well): the

small number of dispensers of news, information, and entertainment in Japan is remarkable in a country with half the population of America. Substantial advocates of individual or minority causes do not exist—at least not on a mass-market basis. Without conscious thought or effort, the programs reflect what people feel, who in turn dictate what the programs will show (which will reflect what people feel), and so on. It is both the curse and comfort of a basically homogeneous society. Op-ed pages are included in newspapers, but the very fact that someone will make the effort to come up with an opinion contrary to the feelings of the masses by itself tends to damage credibility. Nowhere else in life—home, school, or employment—is anyone encouraged to take the opposing stance.

Japan is wrestling with the problem of becoming, as they say, "internationally minded." The system, however, reinforces insular behavior. That is relatively harmless—it just makes the "internationalization" process take longer—but think how efficiently "control" can really be established. (But only, it goes without saying, if necessary.)

· Advertising ·

Question: A man sits on the beach in a folding camp chair. The ocean ripples in the golden reflection of a setting sun. A dog at his side, the man sips reflectively from a glass of amber liquid—his head slightly bobbing, apparently in time with the music playing on his headset. The music of Bach fills the soundtrack. He crosses one denim-clad leg over the other, raises his glass, and offers a silent toast to the camera. The camera pans back, and seagulls swoop and soar over the man's head. A voice announces the name of the product. What is being advertised in this Japanese television commercial?

Answer: Stomach medicine. (You see, the man wouldn't

be having such a wonderful time if he were back in his room whooping it up down the toilet.)

• • •

Question: A sophisticated young woman in a translucent negligee sits at the grand piano in a sun-drenched room bigger than anything possible in Japan. She rises, floats gracefully to the picture window, and gazes in soft focus at the cherry blossoms in the garden. Behind her, a lion appears at the top of the marble stairs, looks around, and pads down to the main room. He again looks around, and then (so help me God) slinks over and sniffs the piano bench. What, be careful now, is being advertised in this Japanese television commercial?

Answer: (And this one should be obvious.) A home burglar alarm system.

• • •

Question: A former baseball star and later manager of a championship team stands in a room while a contemporary jazz great shows him how to hold a saxophone. After several false starts (with laughter in the background), the former baseball star and later manager of a championship team succeeds in creating two bleats on the horn. What is being advertised in this Japanese television commercial?

Answer: (Yoooou got it!) Credit cards.

• • •

The thrust of Japanese advertising is intended to create in the prospective customer a feeling of goodwill, confidence, and trust in the company and product without going into the details of the product's specific use or application. It's as if everything's a tampon commercial. (Although *that* product, relatively new to Japan, is one that oddly enough the advertisers believe requires an element of instruction so that usage becomes accepted. Your author leaves the room when the little line drawing—much like the old Alka-Seltzer diagrams showing relief going down to the stomach and up to the head—flashes on the screen.)

Whereas AMERI-THINK believes the "sell" should be hard, with the advertised product shown beating the pants off the competition, JAPAN-THINK believes that creating an aura of "good feeling" is what makes people buy and come back again. (The frustration level of American creative directors in Japan is understandably high—not unlike that of a snake with a six-shooter strapped to his hips.) The Japanese, however, will go out of their way to avoid a direct confrontation. Remember the example of how business decisions are made and the fact that no one will say too much at first. Coming right out in flat opposition of someone or something is not done. It's a "jarring" note, and that creates nothing but bad feelings in an otherwise harmonious society.

AMERI-AD: "Oh, Don, hee, hee, the pile of clothes washed with *this* soap—in the blue box with a red circle around its three-letter name—looks like it was rinsed in river-bottom mud. *Your* soap, however, makes the other pile so bright and fresh it hurts my eyes."

JAPAN-AD: "Well, here we are. One happy family out riding the Ferris wheel, feeding the swans, and buying cute little dolls (stuffed). Look how funny Daddy looks with cotton candy in his hair. Next, we're going to have nine hours of uninterrupted fun in the car fighting traffic all the way home." (*And,* says the voice-over, *it's all made possible by Mitsubishi Soap.*)

One exception to all the above, it is fair to report, is the increasing direct competition between and among companies marketing New Age consumer electronics and personal computers in Japan. There is no "tradition" behind advertising these products, and gaining market share is so crucial that the stops, by Japanese standards, are being pulled out. No one goes head-to-head, but Sony points out that its video camera can be hidden behind a passport, Sanyo claims its laptop computer is so light it won't wrinkle your trousers, and the phone company's new fax will fit in your hat. This is radical stuff, and it may be ushering in a new era for commercial fans.

Because television and newsprint are effectively national in scope, and because the raw numbers in the market are divided by relatively few competitors, advertising in major media can reach people numbering in the tens of millions. One, therefore, doesn't find Honest Sam Sakai flogging used cars on television or the local supermarket putting discount coupons in the newspaper. The powerful advertising agencies buy all media space, and only the very rich corporations can afford the rates. Toyota, Honda, Panasonic, Sony, and companies in that category all advertise in all the major media. Flipping through channels during prime-time television, for example, one might find the same Suntory whiskey ads all on at the same time. The specific ratings for a specific program is the responsibility of the producer more concerned about its popularity for aesthetic reasons (ha, that's a good one) rather than just financial reasons.

· The Blitz of Media ·

How, you ask, do Honest Sam Sakai and several million of his fellow merchants and businessmen not able to afford big-time advertising get to the buyers? It is difficult to count the ways.

In addition to the national and regional newspapers mentioned previously, there are more than sixty local papers published in various regions of Japan—some with circulations as low as fifteen to twenty thousand—which concentrate on local news or serve as "shoppers' guides" for clusters of towns and villages.

There are twelve daily sports newspapers.

There are several hundred weekly and monthly magazines, most directed at target markets—new brides, new graduates, new mothers, new teens, new adults, new fashion-conscious, new studs, new gays, new race drivers, new car owners, new home owners, new dressmakers, new cooks, plus twenty-three specifically in the sports and leisure group. (These include, in addition to seven golf magazines, publications directed to FM owners, holiday takers, and television watchers.)

There are over a quarter million buses, subways, and train cars capable of "postering" anywhere from sixty to one hundred ads per car.

There are almost a half million taxicabs with back-of-the-front-seat ad space and "take-one" pouches. (One back-of-the-front-seat ad campaign in Tokyo several years ago missed the mark—at least to those of the Christian inclination. A reproduction of Leonardo's *Last Supper,* complete with balloon captions, had the assemblage discussing the merits of the food and wine at Suzuki's Italian restaurant.)

There are umpteen fire hydrants (with great regret, your author was not able to find out the exact number) in Japan. Most are marked by a tall metal pole painted red (so that the hydrants can be seen behind parked automobiles). The tops of the poles curve over and support a metal disk the size of a serving plate. On one side, the disk says "Fire Hydrant." The other side is commercial space—used mostly by insurance companies and house-rental agencies.

There are 89,554,291 telephone poles in Japan. (Your author, frustrated by not getting the exact number of fire hydrants, went out one afternoon and counted the telephone poles.) From knee level to the wires, the poles support as many as a dozen ads each for neighborhood businesses such as rental agencies (again), restaurants, nightclubs, Sakai-san's used cars, and "escort" services.

There are, at any given time, hundreds of cute college girls in short dresses out on the streets giving away tissues, cigarettes, phone cards, or street maps—courtesy of a merchant or businessman in the neighborhood.

There are "billboard trucks" whose only function is to contribute to traffic congestion and advertise the products represented on their sides. The most effective ones have a loudspeaker system magnifying the screechings of girls touting brands of pantyhose, record albums, or after-shave lotion.

There are public address systems in most department stores (some of them coordinated with huge video screens on the wall) indicating the counters of merchandise where discount sales will be staged (until those counters fill up and "sales" are announced elsewhere).

There are four manned blimps and perhaps as many remote-control blimps that float overhead flashing brand names for one and all to see. Their efforts are augmented by skywriters and small planes dragging banners.

There are wandering trash collectors (who exchange old newspapers and magazines for new toilet paper) with amplified but recorded voices shouting their services. Their trucks advertise other products.

There are sweet potato and chestnut roasters (on open fires) who drive around in their portable ovens shouting their wares at ear-splitting decibel levels. (Their trucks also advertise other products.)

There are more lights, signs, flashing announcements, and electrical displays in the Ginza, Roppongi, Shinjuku, Shibuya, Akasaka, Ikebukuro, or Asakusa (and that's just Tokyo) than there ever were in the heyday of Broadway's Great White Way. Every display is selling something.

Coupled with direct mail (an infant but growing industry in Japan); newspaper, mailbox, and magazine stuffers; company bulletins and announcements; street-corner product demonstrations; loudspeakered advertising jingles; commercials before feature films at the movies; and vending machines that automatically talk when people pass, the Japanese have more information thrown at them than any group of people in history. The word "blitz" does not adequately describe the situation.

AMERI-THINK: "Let's saturate the market, it'll improve our share."
JAPAN-THINK: "Saturate the market? Let me know when it's over. I'm going to bed."

Chapter

16

· · ·

POLITICAL MATTERS

The arrival of Commodore Perry's black ships signaled the "official" opening of Japan, and the lives of Jiro and his colleagues were changed forever. The "Tokugawa government"—a dictatorship of some 250 years started by a shogun named Tokugawa—had effectively pushed the imperial family aside and consigned them to generations of "temple life" and occasional ceremonial duties. (So much for the theory that the emperor and his descendants had always been the one and only infallible "god.")

By banning all contact with foreigners, the shoguns succeeding Tokugawa were able to keep the population under control and away from radical ideas which might lead to a resumption of the civil wars that brought the shogunate to power in the first place. Interestingly, even the Japanese who wandered off and had contact with foreigners—usually fishermen caught in storms and winding up in St. Louis, or some such incredible thing—were to be shunned upon their return and condemned to outcast status.

Several things were beginning to change by the mid-nineteenth century, however. Isolation was impossible to maintain with foreign ships—often American whalers—showing up in the northern islands of Japan demanding water and fresh food. Traders and merchants from Southeast Asia, despite the ban on their presence, would travel to the southern islands of Japan and deal in silk and pottery. European ships, doing an increasing business with China, would be "blown off course" almost on a regular basis and find themselves in Japanese ports seeking business. A number of governments had made overtures to the Tokugawa government to allow the official establishment of port facilities for "traders in transit."

On the domestic side, although Japan was still overwhelmingly and predominantly a rural, agricultural society, Jiro most certainly had cousins working in palace cities like Osaka, Kyoto, and Edo (now Tokyo). There, merchants, shopkeepers, craftsmen, and traders—originally positioned to serve the needs of the Tokugawa palaces—were building independent businesses and agitating for new markets for their products. Candles, ornamental hairpins, tortoiseshell products, writing utensils, and woven clothing were now being produced for the masses, not just the nobility. Admiral Perry visited Jiro's village *not* to conquer anything. He represented the American government in effect seeking trading rights. And look what God hath wrought.

The collapse of shogunate rule and the reestablishment of power to the emperor took place fourteen years after Perry's arrival. Meiji, rescued from a life of studying ancient scrolls in the temple and long periods of rock-garden contemplation, proved to be one of the most remarkable leaders in Japanese history. As emperor, Meiji moved the seat of government from western Japan and the old power base to the relatively raucous city of Edo (which he renamed "Tokyo"). He then proceeded to direct the nation on a "crash course" designed to catch up to the rest of the world. He sent students abroad, he hired foreign engineers, scientists, and teachers, and commissioned studies on political reorganization. By the beginning of the twentieth century, the sons of people like Jiro were wearing Western clothes, reading blueprints, and debating the pros and cons of parliamentarian forms of government.

To put this in perspective, Meiji and his policies dragged, cajoled, encouraged, and boosted people like Jiro's son to abandon the life of what Westerners would consider medieval feudalism, and to move from a peasant mentality to one prepared to accept and challenge the demands of the "modern" world. Emperor Meiji died in 1912. His grandson, Hirohito, was the one who died in 1989. And it is the grandson of Jiro's son who is today's minister of finance, chairman of Mitsubishi, or prime minister. It has been a very long journey in a very short time.

The constitution drafted by American Occupation authorities and accepted by the Japanese was less of a revolutionary document at that time to the Japanese than the American Constitution was to Americans in 1789. Beginning with the Meiji era, a framework of self-government existed wherein power resided in a leadership of people acknowledged as being "responsible"—barons, landowners, titled individuals, as well as commoners involved in education, business, and military affairs. There were prime ministers, ministers of major governmental functions, and an organized forum (the Diet) for debate and discussion. The emperor was the official "head" of government, but his role was not spelled out, and as a practical matter he abdicated his presumed authority to those involved in the daily business of running the country. (What happened during World War II, and the emperor's role in it all, will probably be debated forever. Whether he led, followed, supported, or opposed the war effort is difficult to determine because of the complexity of *all* issues in and around a nation at war. It *is* clear, however, that the war was waged in his name.) The new postwar constitution separated the emperor from government, and established the power and authority of government in *all* the people in a representative system. Enter the politicians.

Americans have had over two hundred years to get used to the idea of electing someone to act as a representative, bidding the representative farewell and Godspeed for the journey to the government center, and then sitting back and watching the representative turn into a blithering idiot, a brilliant statesman, or a convicted felon. The advantage Americans have with this long history is that both sides—the representer and the representee—have firm ideas as to the role each plays.

Japan is another matter. Since the dawn of history, or at least as far back as anyone or their grandparents can remember, the government has been run by bureaucrats—henchmen of the boss. Politicians are . . . what?

AMERI-THINK: "I saw *my* congressman on television last night, and I'm going to give him a piece of my mind. I'm writing to him, and if he doesn't get behind dairy supports, he'll be running his next campaign with play money."

JAPAN-THINK: "I saw the Diet member from, I think, our district on television last night. He must be working too hard—he was asleep."

To further complicate matters in Japan, there's no boss. Americans have a President, and subject to the checks and balances of Congress and the Supreme Court, he establishes the game plan and works toward accomplishing the goals for which he was elected in the political process. The power of the people sort of flows on a direct basis (despite the hocus-pocus of the electoral college) up to his level. That ain't the case in Japan.

Based more closely on the British system (but without the long history of England's representative form of government), the reigning political party elects the prime minister of Japan. It's accepted that people coming into power through *that* route aren't in charge of Japan. They're not bureaucrats, and compared to the good old days, they're not . . . well, the boss.

If you'll recall, Japan made a conscious decision after the devastation of war to rebuild and reconstruct as quickly and efficiently as possible. "Political" matters were back-burner stuff; the *real* shaping of things to come was fashioned by the alliance of business and government. And "government" meant the people in charge of granting licenses, permissions, right-of-ways, and exemptions, as well as imposing restrictions, controls, and limitations. Bureaucrats.

Question: When does a bureaucrat make an individual decision? Not often, you say? That may be true when a bureaucrat is a bureaucrat. But in Japan (remember how hard those mothers hustled to get their kids into the "right schools") the bureaucrats "descend from heaven" upon retirement and land smack dab in the lucrative heart of business. And decisions have a way of being made.

(Would a former bureaucrat now employed by a major business entity in Japan go back and visit his former colleagues with foot-stomping, arm-waving demands? Of course not—that would be crude. But over a civilized cup of tea, or perhaps during a civilized dinner after work, the sudden in-rush of breath, the knitted brow, the subtle fidgeting of impatience—

so familiar to the bureaucrat who after thousands of hours of faithful service to the man across the table has brought him to his current position in the first place—the "sense" of the issue becomes crystal clear.)

Those people run Japan. The problem is, external matters must go through the politicians.

Your author, rummaging through heretofore restricted postwar archives, has come up with a dust-covered document in which minutes of the first postwar political meeting in Japan were detailed. As permission has not yet been obtained for the publication of these chronicles, it would be appreciated if the following be kept in strict confidence:

"Cannot have two parties. Cannot be. This is Japan."

"But," cautioned Yoshida-san, "new constitution, compliments of our new American friends and former sworn enemies, indicates open election, heh, heh, heh, excuse me, for public leaders."

"How can we have two parties? We can only agree by all sitting together in one room, forming factions, compromising positions, smoking cigarettes, broker-ing power, sucking wind, punishing recalcitrants, and putting up candidates. If not all in same party, how can we do that?"

"I'm just saying we must have opposition for elec-tions."

(Yoshida-san's notes on the affair indicate he was not happy with his assignment. To ask otherwise sensible and traditional Japanese to go off by themselves—all alone—and compete head-to-head in public forum was sheer madness. Winning would be bad enough—impolite and all that—but *then* what would happen? No support from an organization would be like trying to get a rice crop in all by oneself.)

   "Hey, wait a minute. You may have hit on something."
   "I have?" asked Yoshida-san.
   "Opposition. You said it yourself. We'll make the *appearance* of opposition. Then everyone will be satisfied."

And that, ladies and gentlemen, is how the Liberal Democratic Party—the ruling party since the war—was formed. The last people in the room that day were given the assignment of forming the other parties, from and because of which factions can be formed, positions can be compromised, power can be brokered, and candidates can be put up. That is, of course, if the LDP itself runs out of options in this regard internally.

   Now then, can a Japanese prime minister, visiting America and standing sort of tall in the Oval Office, deliver on the promises extracted from him by the President? Well, picture the problems the President would face if the tables were reversed. ("Look, Lee, I'm asking you to cut production and exports from your Belvidere plant. There's a 20 percent unemployment rate in Maebashi," or, "I know corn is kinda important to you folks in Iowa, but I'd like you to plow under your crops and import rice instead.") Take the President's chances of organizing such a turnabout and then divide by ninety-nine. That will give you an idea of the problems facing the poor bastard who happens to be compromised up to the prime minister's position in Japan.

   The political profession in Japan is not yet the noble profession thought of in America—Senators Snort and Phil A. Buster notwithstanding. Candidates parade around in sound trucks at election time, their pictures are plastered at random and in great quantities on all flat surfaces in the neighborhood, and they now and then will get out and "press the flesh." (Actually, they "press the cotton." For some reason, all candidates wear white cotton gloves. Since gloves are for the dual purpose of keeping warm and protecting against contamination, and since the elections are all held in the warm months, the imagery is unfortunate.) But despite the effort, expectations are low.

> AMERI-THINK: "I don't vote because the candidate *won't* do anything about it."
> JAPAN-THINK: "I don't vote because the candidate *can't* do anything about it."

Chapter

17

. . .

LANGUAGE, AS A VEHICLE FOR MISCOMMUNICATION

Effective communication is often taken for granted. We humans have evolved a marvelous system whereby our throats and mouths—in close cooperation with our tongues and teeth—emit a variety of sounds which, because of an ability to duplicate and repeat these sounds in connection with recognizable behavior patterns, make our innermost thoughts and intentions crystal-clear.

Many living creatures, we are told, communicate within their species. In the lower orders of life, the transfer of information is admittedly limited to the needs of the moment. Fish, for example, are rarely called upon to describe to their households the intricacies involved in setting digital watches or tuning in to CNN. Fish don't wear digital watches (or pay much attention to CNN).

Yet fish, to follow the example, get the idea across to friends and relatives that it's a better idea to swim upstream to spawn than to check into the Hilton Hotel. Birds, bees, and rhinoceri are equally clever at getting their points across to others within their species. Witness the swallows at Capistrano. Or consider bankers when the trust markets open.

Humans, however, bear a special burden in communicating effectively. Not only is our subject matter often more complex than standard gibbon chatter; our facile ability to modify sounds issuing from our throats and mouths has led us off into a multitude of "variations" which we call "languages."

Americans speak a language called "English."

Japanese speak a language called "Japanese."

There are probably not two nations on earth with citizens more inept at speaking a language other than their own than America and Japan. (And we know there are all kinds of excuses for that.) What is one man's *la plume* becomes another man's *Schreibfeder,* but the Americans know damn well that the thing that leaks ink on the fingers is a "ball-point pen." To the Japanese, it's an *enpitsu* because anything else isn't right (and would be too hard to pronounce anyway).

JAPAN-THINK: With all its rules and regulations, English is still the most disorganized language in existence. Consider, say the Japanese, the following:

A. *Plurals* If there are "geese" why aren't there "meese"? If there are "oxen" why aren't there "boxen"? If there are "mice" why aren't there "hice"?

B. *Action* If a singer "sings" why doesn't a finger "fing"? (Or grocer "groce"?) If a vegetarian eats vegetables, what does a humanitarian eat? Why does one ride *in* a car but *on* a train?

C. *Tense* If sing becomes "sang" why doesn't fling become "flang"? A paper can be "wrote" but a sandwich can't be "bote." (And any sentence with any form of the word "lie" must be avoided at all costs.)

D. *Usage* How can "oversight" mean both a mistake and supervision? "Left" means go away or stay behind. One can turn a light "out" but not "in." Why does "dust" mean to dirty something or to clean something? Being "below par" is good in golf but bad in feeling. (And speaking of golf, a big handicap is an advantage.)

The list of bizarre contradictions and curious exceptions in the English language is very long—after all, it's a hybrid language with loan words and adopted grammar. Furthermore, it continues to evolve and change. It's awful, for example. (And for Japanese, more accustomed to learning rules without variations, it's also aweful.)

AMERI-THINK: Learning another language is bad enough, particularly with perfectly good English already invented, but learning a language one must *draw* is next to impossible.

In the good old days, some 1,500 years ago, the Japanese had a perfectly good spoken language adequate to the needs of the time. ("Hey, Yoko, where are the chopsticks?" "Chopsticks? Oh, here they are. I was knitting a sweater.")

So that things could be written down ("I'll be late, dinner's in the oven, and the chopsticks are in the sweater"), Chinese ideographs were adopted and overlaid onto the spoken language. Modifications and adjustments were made over the years, but to this day Japanese and Chinese can look at each other's ideographs and generally understand the meaning of the picture but not the spoken language that goes with the picture. (Yoko's note would consist of the standard picture for "late," "a cooking dinner," "chopsticks," and "sweater"— not necessarily in that order, by the way—plus little modifiers in between to prevent her husband from misunderstanding, eating the sweater and going out late with the oven and the chopsticks.)

It involves a different thought process to look at a picture and have a specific meaning flash into the brain compared to the linear approach of words and action flowing along to a conclusion logical to Americans. But thought processes are relatively easy to adjust. What is not easy is sitting down and *memorizing* the meaning of 2,000 pictures just to gain minimum fluency, and another couple of thousand or so for intercourse in polite society. (To add to this remarkable situation, it's not enough to just memorize the meaning of all the pictures; one must also remember how to *draw* them to be considered literate.)

> JAPAN-THINK: "What could be simpler than learning by rote four or five thousand characters—each with a dozen or so strokes? It's easier than tiptoeing through the minefields of sentences like 'I flang the ball, hitted the woman, and laid her on the desk.'"
> AMERI-THINK: "Are you kidding me? And why the desk?"

Miscommunication can occur between the best of friends speaking in a native and common language. ("I said I *saw* your husband, I didn't say I'm *seeing* him.") The chances of miscommunication increase with every step away from the common hearth. The differences between British and American English are well chronicled ("I'm stepping out for a fag"), but by the time we enter the realm of second languages, communication and miscommunication becomes a fifty-fifty proposition. (When asked by a virginal young lady if her dress was attractive, your author replied with avuncular warmth in his best Japanese that he was "horny." That situation notwithstanding, it should be pointed out that the phrase "color-blind" is represented by the word "shikimo." The phrase "passionately aroused" is represented by the word "shikima."

All that fuss—screeching, recriminations, and humble apologies—over one teeny-tiny nondescript vowel at the end of a word.)

Americans without Japanese fluency (one teeny-tiny vowel!) would be wise adhering to the following basic rules when attempting communication. Nothing is guaranteed, of course, but it should maintain the communication/miscommunication dichotomy at about fifty-fifty.

1. *Be careful of colloquialisms.* Telling a Japanese businessman that the reason you are late for the important meeting is because taxis were scarce due to the condition of the weather is fine. That's understandable. One American, however, went too far. At the end of the meeting—a meeting during which the Japanese businessman did little more than stare icily at the American—the final good-byes revealed the problem. "I hope your pets get dry," said the Japanese businessman in parting. ("Pets get dry"?) It later dawned on the American that he had mentioned upon arrival that "it was raining cats and dogs."

2. *Easy does it.* "Your wife is dead," said the note handed to the American by a Japanese secretary. "Please call up to your friend," it concluded. After a half hour of sheer panic and frantic calls around town, the American found and spoke to his wife. She was *not* dead. As he was staring in a daze at the note in his hand, the phone rang. "Didn't you get my message?" said the friend in his rapid-fire speaking style. "I told the secretary to ask you to call me before lunch. I told her it was a matter of life and death."

3. *Be particularly explicit with instructions.* "Photocopy the paper-clipped pages," instructed the new American in Japan. He had been up most of the night before,

reading through corporate manuals. Several hundred pages of particularly key information were to be condensed for the benefit of the local staff. The paper clips were to separate the wheat from the chaff, so to speak. The clerk assigned to the job could not really be faulted. The sequence of words, unfortunately, just didn't register properly. (Remember, she was more accustomed to ideas flashing into her brain all at once.) After twenty minutes she returned with . . . a page of photocopied paper clips—carefully removed from the manuals and reproduced.

AMERI-THINK demands a clear "yes" or "no" when that's what the question asks for. (If an American wants a long, convoluted answer, he'll ask about the weather.) "Yes or no, isn't this the best idea since sliced bread?"

JAPAN-THINK knows that things are never so extreme as "yes" or "no." There *is* a word for "yes" in Japan—"hai"—and it's heard in conversation quite a bit. But it does not represent a direct answer to a direct question. It is used in the sense of "Yes, I understand your question," or "Yes, I know you would dearly love an answer to that," but never in the sense "Yes, you can bet your boots that's the best idea since sliced bread—or even better." (The number of Americans who have left Japan thinking they had a deal when they heard the word "yes"—only later to find out it meant something else—would, if laid end-to-end, reach from Tokyo to New York. In fact, they do.) There is no "no" in Japan. It would hurt too many feelings. And it's not really necessary. (People go away after a while anyway.)

AMERI-THINK believes that communication is primarily verbal or written. Gestures—pounding the desk, stomping the foot, or pulling the necktie up in a mock gesture of being hanged—are merely punctuation points to accompany speech. ("I want to make one thing perfectly clear—bang—if we don't hit the ground running on this—stomp, stomp—we're gonna see the share price drop fifty points—argggghh.")

JAPAN-THINK considers written or verbal communication to be only part of the communication process. Of almost equal importance are the waves of feedback and information flowing from stomach to stomach as the result of subtle twitchings, purrs of content or disagreement, sudden inrushes of air through clenched teeth, and the assumption of various poses (as in the pose of being asleep or the pose of being awake). The last time anyone used gestures approaching Western flamboyance was when war was declared (a desk was pounded in the Diet building), a description of losses in the South Pacific was made (stomping was heard from the direction of Naval Command), and war criminals were brought to trial (argggghh). Within the homogeny that is Japan, a flickering eyelid tells all.

AMERI-THINK believes it is important to communicate the essentials "up front," starting with name, rank, and serial number. ("Hi, there. I'm Jack from Kansas City. I'm an engineer and build rockets and things.") Greetings can actually begin from halfway across the room.

JAPAN-THINK has developed an elaborate ritual surrounding the introductory process. Let's suppose two old friends, Mr. A and Mr. B, meet in a restaurant. With each man is another man, Mr. X and Mr. Y. Mr. X and Mr. Y are strangers to each other. All four will sit down at the table, and Mr. A and Mr. B will exchange pleasantries and perhaps share a private joke. Mr. X and Mr. Y will studiously ignore each other as well as either Mr. A or Mr. B who is also a stranger to them. (If this is becoming too complicated, I'll slow down.) Finally, when everyone is settled and a mood is established, either Mr. A or Mr. B (whoever between *them* is more junior) will suddenly exclaim as if in surprise (and as if it slipped his mind): "Ho, ha, I'm sorry. I don't think you know my friend here." Everyone stands, formal introductions begin, a flurry of business cards crisscrosses the table, and deep bows are performed. From that moment on, but *only* from that moment on, the members of the group can laugh and joke, tell stories, and discover that they're either all from the same school or related by marriage. But none of this "Hi, there. I'm Jack" stuff from across the room.

AMERI-THINK believes silence is a vacuum into which sound, any sound, should be introduced.

> AMERICAN: "Don't you agree that our widgets are pretty damn phenomenal?"
> JAPANESE: (Silence)
> AMERICAN: "I mean, priced the way they are. A little expensive, but, you know, labor costs."
> JAPANESE: (Silence)
> AMERICAN: "Actually, we could reduce the price a little."
> JAPANESE: (Silence)
> AMERICAN: "But then quality would suffer. We're already having problems with some of the batches."
> JAPANESE: (Silence)
> AMERICAN: "Well, we *could* give them to you, but then we'd want to negotiate a healthy commission for our side based on your sales."
> JAPANESE: (Silence)
> AMERICAN: "Okay, Watanabe-san. You drive a hard bargain. We'll *pay* you to sell these for us, but, er, let's talk about if we get anything out of the deal."

JAPAN-THINK recognizes that the same negotiation can take place between two wave-lengthed Japanese in the following fashion.

JAPANESE #1: "Widgets?"
JAPANESE #2: "Umph."
JAPANESE #1: (Silence)
JAPANESE #2: "Sssssih." (The old-inrush-of-air-between-clenched-teeth maneuver.)
JAPANESE #1: "Price."
JAPANESE #2: "So des ne."
JAPANESE #1: (Twitch)
JAPANESE #2: "Haaaaa." (Spoken gutturally)
JAPANESE #1: (Silence)
JAPANESE #2: "Teats."
JAPANESE #1: "Ass."
JAPANESE #2: "Heh, heh, heh."
JAPANESE #1: "Heh, heh, heh."
JAPANESE #2: (Silence)
JAPANESE #1: "Cost."
JAPANESE #2: "Oooohh."
JAPANESE #1: "Maybe we have deal."

And in Japan, "maybe we have deal" is the kind of iron-clad agreement that has bound business entities together since long before Jiro came on the scene.

Perhaps a word or two should be said about *circuitous answers* to direct questions. The ability to do this—to come up with the right remark at the right time—has saved faces, marriages, and lives.

ANGRY WIFE: "Where the hell have you been? It's 2:00 A.M. and you smell like a brewery." (Note the directness of the question.)
CONTRITE HUSBAND: "The car broke down, and I luckily got a ride home in a beer truck." (Note the circuity of the answer. *Where* the poor man has been is deftly avoided in this technique.)

CALIFORNIA HIGHWAY PATROLMAN: "Where are you going, Bud, a fire?" (Again, a careful parsing of the sentence will reveal its directness.)
BELEAGUERED MOTORIST: "It's a rented car, officer, and I'm not familiar with the speedometer's location." (The chances are one in a million that the answer will suffice, but that's better than answering "Yes" to the fire question when *that* answer never suffices—unless one is a fire chief.)

Now then, no matter how skillfully this technique is practiced in America, the Japanese have managed to elevate the art of indirectness to levels unsurpassed (or unimagined) in the rest of the world. As an international community service, your author presents the following translations of circuitous answers to standard questions. Communication!

QUESTION: "When are you going to open the rice market to American producers?"
ANSWER: "*We* are still studying the issue."
TRANSLATION: "*We* are still studying the issue" means "Absolutely never if we can get away with it. Once we stop supporting rice farmers, their fields will be plowed under, apartment buildings housing a quarter-million people per acre will be built, and if America ever changes its mind about selling us rice—which after all is not only our staff of life but is the foundation of our culture (and figures prominently in many of our quasi-religious ceremonies)—we'll never be able to displace all those people, tear down those apartment buildings, convince the farmers to return from their palatial estates in Hawaii and begin walking around in the mud to start growing rice again."

QUESTION: "Why are you ignoring Paul Harvey's advice and continuing to vacillate on the 'joining-the-world-peacekeeping-effort' so ardently embraced by other free nations of the world?"

ANSWER: "We *are* still studying the issue."

TRANSLATION: "We *are* still studying the issue" means "Memories are long in the Orient. It's only been recently that nations in our neighborhood trust us enough to allow us to set up offices and trading companies to help alleviate our raw-material problems, since those are the very same countries we raped and pillaged within living memory. Our pacifist constitution, which incidentally was a gift from America, prohibits (to our neighbors' relief) forming and sending an army abroad. As to changing the constitution on that very point, there are still enough right-wing boneheads around who could make the issue one of pro or con constitution period. Most normal Japanese are afraid of that—still not completely trusting us political leaders—so we're caught between the rock and the hard place. Besides, we're not really certain who's in charge here anyway."

QUESTION: "Is there no end to Japanese purchases of American real estate and related landmarks?"

ANSWER: "We are *still* studying the issue."

TRANSLATION: "We are *still* studying the issue" means "The combination of incredible land prices and a painfully archaic tax law *drives* people overseas with their investments since (A) selling land and keeping cash in Japan reduces one from a millionaire on paper to a pauper in practice, and (B) a 5 percent return on real estate investments overseas is better than a return of less than 1 percent in Japan. Given the same amount of money, is one better purchasing land for a two-family income-producing apartment building in Tokyo, or a one-thousand-family income-producing housing development in the hills outside San Diego?"

QUESTION: "If land prices are the problem, why aren't they lowered? It's a restraint of trade when American supermarket chains and Toys 'R' Us can't afford to set up shop in Japan."
ANSWER: "We are still *studying* the issue."
TRANSLATION: "We are still *studying* the issue" means "Get serious. How does one control supply and demand?"

QUESTION: "Isn't it unfair when Japan has free access directly to our markets and yet Japan maintains a complicated distribution process?"
ANSWER: "We are still studying *the* issue."
TRANSLATION: "We are still studying *the* issue" means "probably. But how do we bypass a distributorship system employing roughly 35 percent of our working population—men, women, and children scurrying around like beavers in the time-honored tradition of accepting goods (from someone else who has accepted goods) and in turn delivering them by truck, car, and bicycle to other people who accept them and in turn hustle off to make certain that mom-and-pop stores by the tens of thousands have enough items on the shelf for the weekend? A few bucks' extra cost to the end consumer spread across the board beats an unemployment rate of 35 percent."

QUESTION: "Are Japanese nothing more than mere 'economic animals'?"

ANSWER: "We are still studying the *issue*."
TRANSLATION: "We are still studying the *issue*"
means "No. Remember the Sunday afternoons in the
park with the family."

A final word or two about the construction of language
and the understanding of vocabulary. Take, for example, the
sentence "I am going to the bathroom." It's a perfectly good
sentence to Americans—direct, concise, and to the point. The
"I" in the sentence is the subject, and refers to the speaker.
"Am going" refers to the action the "I" person contemplates.
"To the bathroom" tells us *where* the "I" person "am going."
(*What* the "I" person does upon arrival at the destination is
generally understood but certainly not dwelled upon.)

A Japanese student of the English language, no matter
how poorly he did in high school, will at least have heard of
the words "I," "am," "going," "to," "the," "bathroom." He
probably won't have heard them in the context employed by
the American speaker, however. The word "I" is one of those
things—pronouns—that don't really exist in Japanese. (Per-
sons and things are referred to by their proper names. For
example, the "I" person in Japanese is really "humble serv-
ant," "exalted leader," or "fellow equal" depending upon who
he's talking to.) But that's not a big problem—the Japanese
will have heard "I" enough from Americans to conclude that
it's an all-purpose word covering more subtle distinctions.

"Am going" is one of those forms Americans use to describe what is happening at the present time. "Am writing,"
"am talking," "am breathing" are in the same category. All
those things are occurring NOW. "Bathroom" is crystal-clear
to a Japanese. He has spent quite a bit of time in one. It's
the place one goes to bathe.

A Japanese waiter serving a table of Americans in a restaurant might overhear the sentence "I am going to the bath-

room" as he's serving the pats of butter. He will first conclude that the American has a screw loose. "Am eating" is what the American is doing, not "am going."

If he gets over that hurdle in his mind and assumes that contrary to all the rules he's laboriously memorized, "am going" refers to something happening not now but slightly in the future, he's a step ahead of things. Of more significance, however, is the fact that the waiter knows there's not a bathroom within five kilometers of the restaurant. He takes his butter pats and retreats to a far corner of the restaurant. He has heard about Americans using the euphemism "bathroom" for acts of urination and defecation, and if he's wrong about the slightly future tense of "am going," that table is the last place he'd want to be when the manager finds out about it.

Keeping it simple is the best rule in any kind of communication. Miscommunication can occur between the best of friends speaking in a native and common language. Add to that all the exceptions to rules, incorrectly pronounced words (one teeny-tiny vowel), double meanings, different thought processes, and the 24,000 pen strokes in several thousand ideographs, and it's a wonder there's any communication at all. With that in mind, select the better of the following:

> "Excuse me my good fellow. I'm terribly sorry to bother you while you are so skillfully flipping those butter pats onto the plate, but I wonder if you'd be ever so kind as to point me in the direction of the bathroom?"

> or

"Toilet, where?"

· Animal Language ·

As a service to international farmers and pet owners, animals "say" the following in America and in Japan.

	AMERICA	JAPAN
Dog	"bow-wow" (or "arf")	"one one"
Cat	"meeow"	"nya nya"
Cow	"moo"	"mau"
Frog	"ribbit"*	"kero kero"
Rooster	"cock-a-doodle-do"	"cokekokko"
Birdie	"tweet tweet"	"piyo piyo" or "pi-chiku pachiku"
Crow	"caw"	"ka ka"
Mouse/rat	"squeak" or "SQUEAK"	"chu chu"
Goose	"honk"	"ga ga"
Sheep	"baa"	"me me"
Monkey	(beats me)	"ki ki"
Horse	"neigh"	"hihi-n"

This could go on forever—and remember these creatures also "do" things. Rabbits go "hippity-hop" in America. In Japan, they go "pyong-pyong." (You wouldn't believe what monkeys do.)

*Except in the Mother West Wind stories—there the frogs said "chug-a-rump."

Chapter
18
. . .

FEELING GOOD

The AMERI-THINK response to the little things that now and then go wrong with the body is as follows:

CONDITION	TREATMENT
cut finger	Band-Aid
headache	aspirin
stubbed toe	curses and aspirin
scraped knee	disinfectant and Band-Aid
sprained ankle	cold compresses, later hot ones
tired, scratchy eyes	eyedrops
cold	aspirin, plenty of fluids, tissues
broken arm	visit doctor, in and out same day
pneumonia	visit doctor, bed rest, pills, chicken noodle soup

broken leg

could spend the night in hospital, could be in traction at home, certainly some crutch action

broken gall bladder

operation, hospital stay as long as three to five days

The JAPAN-THINK approach to the disorders is as follows:

CONDITION

TREATMENT

cut finger

hospital, professional bandage from elbow to tip of finger, thirteen varieties of pills, half day off work, revisit hospital every day for the next five days

headache

hospital, brain scan, eight varieties of pills, complete day off work, eye checkup next day

stubbed toe

hospital (overnight), X-rays, fourteen pills, two days off work, cane, professional bandage encasing entire foot and ankle

scraped knee

hospital, antibiotic pills of every color in the spectrum, revisit hospital daily for two weeks for redressing bandage; continue wearing knee pad until end of Rainy Season

sprained ankle

see "stubbed toe" above, except walking cast, one week off work, and six more pills

tired, scratchy eyes	hospital, four types of prescribed eyedrops (depending upon time of day), sixteen varieties of pills, a great, whopping white eye patch (worn on alternate days), no time off work (except for daily hospital visits) but sit around office all day doing things alternately one-handed
cold	badge of honor is white face mask, worn until gray, and thirty-seven liters of green tea per day until next birthday
broken arm	rarely happens (Japanese tend to have shorter, thicker bones) but when it does, gangbusters: hospital confinement for three weeks, intravenous feeding, a banquet of pills (equal otherwise to one square meal), trip to Hawaii to recuperate
pneumonia	hospital (by ambulance), one-month confinement, tests every day for tuberculosis, white face mask until next birthday
broken leg	see "broken arm" except hospital confinement until end of year, crutches until spring; will take pills until end of life

broken gall bladder

hospital, operation, rumors as to whether or not it's cancer ("since doctors don't tell patients that they have cancer, the fact that the patient says he *doesn't* have cancer means the doctor told him he doesn't which means he probably *does* have it but the doctor told him he doesn't"), confinement until eldest child graduates from high school, plastic surgery to fix the stitch marks, medical leave of absence from work until "bonus season," admonitions about ever eating Western food again, recuperation at Disneyland in California

It is quite possible the alert reader will discern a subtle difference in approaches between Japanese and Americans toward health care. Part of it is attitude—a macho-American is not really interested in allowing relative strangers to poke and prod parts of the body that may not be perfect but have proven serviceable down through the years. ("What do you mean, my toes are crooked? I *like* them crooked.") (Your author's father, once told by his doctor—a man twenty years his junior—that it was "inadvisable" to get on an airplane and fly to Seattle, returned from his trip to learn that his doctor had died of a heart attack in the interim. That sequence of events was gleefully recounted at family card parties until the death of your author's father—ten years later.)

The Japanese attitude is an interesting commentary on accepted roles in society. Doctors are learned specialists in their field—their technological expertise is way beyond that of the common man—and not only must "respect" be paid to them; the mere act of questioning their judgment is unthinkable. "Going to the doctor" to obtain guidance and instruction on *any* matter of health and physical welfare is as natural as going to the Ministry of Finance to seek permission to form a joint venture. It is not unusual for otherwise educated people in Japan to significantly alter their life-styles because "a doctor told me to"—and yet it does not occur to anyone to ask "why?" ("My doctor told me to stop eating chicken, stop riding on airplanes, and stop wearing red neckties.") AMERI-THINK might be inclined to get a second opinion—particularly about the red neckties. JAPAN-THINK wouldn't dream of it. If someone "higher" in the structure says to do something, that something must be done.

But there is also another good reason for the Japanese approach to medical care. "Consultation" costs about as much as a cup of coffee and a slice of pie. American private insurance policies, with deductibles sometimes equal to one year's salary, provide benefits payable in formulae similar to those used to track the Pioneer spacecraft combined with odds calculations built in to "one-arm bandits" in Las Vegas. ("We agree that you were hit by a car on Main Street, but it was going the wrong way on a one-way street, it was between the hours of dusk and dawn, and your shirttail was out.")

It is difficult to argue with the Japanese system when one considers the life expectancy of the population. Clearly, "preventive maintenance" works in other areas. ("If you don't spend ten dollars to change your oil filter now, it could cost three thousand dollars when your engine blows up six months from now.")

It is not easy to ascertain the exact cost of delivering medical services in Japan—the government subsidizes the program and collects a "national health insurance" premium

from every citizen. Patients pay mini͏ͅ
treatments. <u>Doctors are paid a salary, bu͏ͅ
by selling medicine. A</u> day without a fist͏ͅ
anese is like a day without sun.

A Japan-U.S. health care symposium ͏ͅ
in Tokyo—the first of what is planned to be a͏ͅ
and different approaches taken by the medical frate͏ͅ
both sides of the Pacific were interesting to observe. ͏ͅ
Americans showed up with autopsy reports, videos of spectacular accomplishments on the operating table, hints of
breakthroughs in curing rare and disturbing diseases, and reports of diagnostic machinery more complicated than spacecraft but no bigger than a breadbox. The Japanese, on the
other hand, concentrated on demonstrations of ambulance
pickup and delivery systems, cost accounting for hospitals,
the condition of medical schools, and the difficulties of col-
lecting insurance claims from foreigners with overseas insurance policies. Perhaps the subject will come up in subsequent
symposiums, but at the first one everybody forgot to mention
issues involving the "treatment of patients."

AMERI-THINK is pretty certain that one is better off if
a hospital is *never* entered—except perhaps to visit some unfortunate wretch too weak or undisciplined to avoid it. ("In
all my fifty years I've only been to a hospital once, and that
was the day I was born.")

JAPAN-THINK knows that only the animals of the forest
don't go to hospitals regularly. (In fact *all* Japanese, young,
old, sick, or healthy, go once a year to "human dock"—an
annual checkup named as such because even ships return to
port once a year for refurbishing.)

AMERI-THINK says that "in and out" is the best
course—the average hospital stay in the States is somewhere
between three and four days.

JAPAN-THINK knows that leaving a hospital too early

special problems. Given the lack of space, conva-
ce is difficult in a multipurpose room at home. The
age hospital stay is fifteen days.

"Mr. American, why are you in the hospital?"
"I'm glad you asked. I've developed hypopara-
thyroidism, a condition resulting from deficiency of
the parathyroid hormone. There's always the possibility of tetany, plus the goddamn intermittent, bi-
lateral muscular spasms which are painful as hell. I'll
be here for a week or so while they try to raise the
calcium level in my blood and reduce the high phos-
phorus level. Want a glass of milk?"

"Mr. Japanese, why are you in the hospital?"
"Because the doctor put me here."

Chapter

19
. . .

YOUR ATTITUDE, OR MINE?

A whole bunch of Japanese and a whole bunch of Americans have rubbed a whole bunch of elbows during the last four decades. Beginning with the U.S. Occupation, there were military people doing their thing in the areas of maintaining security, keeping peace, and directing traffic. At the same time there were countless bureaucrats, civil servants, doctors, lawyers, economists, and linguists on both sides interacting in the business of restructuring the country. (Even Dr. Deming was rubbing elbows.)

Students began exchanging between Japan and America within a year of two of the war's conclusion. It started as a trickle at first—the Fulbright Foundation began funding studies for Japanese going to America in 1952—but it rapidly grew to the wave it is now. It is variously estimated that at any given time there are at least a half million Japanese studying something in America—either in the grade schools, high schools, colleges, and universities, or in training programs conducted by employers and joint-venture partners. There are less than half that many Americans studying in Japan (kids from Toledo don't grow up dreaming of someday going to Hitotsubashi University the way their Japanese counterparts dream of going to Harvard), but with all the U.S. military families, business families, missionaries, and thousands of graduate students as well as private students, there are significant numbers of Americans in Japan learning about the people and culture.

The business arena has proven to be a learning ground also. Japanese and American businessmen have together and in each country built things, redesigned things, sold things, and tried to increase market share. With all the intense personnel matters that must be handled, unknowing head office folks that must be educated, and the puzzles of customer demands that must be solved, there is a whole bunch of international elbow-rubbing going on.

What is remarkable is that if Americans and British, Americans and Germans, even Americans and French peoples were thrown together in such concentrated and demanding circumstances, a common language would have probably emerged ("Sie are eine cute petite bird, cherie old kid"), restaurateurs would regularly feature schnitzel flambé with haggis and corn on the cob, and the British would have begun to form friendships outside the circle of old schoolmates.

Yet despite all the educational, social, business, and diplomatic intercourse that has (and is) occurring between Americans and Japanese, there are still interestingly resolute polarities of attitudes.

AMERI-THINK still remembers Pearl Harbor and considers the "sneak attack" as being both a low blow (and not in keeping with the spirit of the game) and perhaps an indication of Japanese untrustworthiness.

JAPAN-THINK often has second thoughts about American consistency and trustworthiness. ("How can we believe them if their company president swears commitment to the project and then quits the company—or allows himself to be fired—two weeks later?")

AMERI-THINK has had it confirmed on many occasions that a Japanese will profess no knowledge of details under discussion but will secretly be an expert in the field.

JAPAN-THINK has had it confirmed on many occasions that an American will boast of expertise of details under discussion but is really either bluffing or trying to con everyone.

AMERI-THINK recognizes the reality that Japan has rapidly become one of the more powerful nations on earth, and as such should take a stand on international issues.

JAPAN-THINK recognizes the reality that other than rainwater it has no natural resources, everything has to be imported and paid for to survive, a stand on international issues is difficult when everyone's still in the meeting to figure out what to do with the traffic problem in Tokyo, and once everyone stops pedaling the bicycle furiously, the Japanese economy will coast to a stop.

AMERI-THINK considers a Japanese to be nothing more than an "economic animal" interested only in structuring a deal to fit his own needs.

JAPAN-THINK considers an American to be more interested in structuring a deal to fit his own needs (and for the benefit of those looking at quarterly reports) than slowing down and establishing ongoing relationships.

AMERI-THINK believes in the concept of individual

leadership which permits one to rise above the whole, take the bull by the horns, and direct efforts toward a logical and beneficial conclusion.

JAPAN-THINK still worries about that—individuals going off on their own are usually oddballs.

At the heart of the matter is the fact that Americans and Japanese quite naturally do what each does best. What one "does best" is a by-product of cultural heritage and education coupled with experiences of success or failure.

Quite obviously, Americans have more in common in terms of cultural heritage with Europeans. Automatic reactions to situations are similar for both instinctual and learned reasons. Taking a step back and looking at it with a slightly broader perspective, the "universal truths" accepted by Americans and Europeans are shaped by heritage, and are in fact not quite as "universal" as one might think. Circumstances and the experiences of success or failure have been similar, and that confirms the worth of the American/European cultural heritage. But that's only one way of looking at it.

The Japanese cultural heritage is radically different. Although much has come to Japan from China, the extraordinary and, at least in "modern" history, unprecedented 250-year isolation just as other nations were bursting forth with new technology and ideas is profoundly important to understanding the situation. Japanese cultural heritage is Japanese, and not in any real sense even Chinese. It developed, was modified to circumstances, and closed in on itself with a centripetal force unlike anything experienced by any significant portion of mankind in a thousand years. Make no bones about it: The Japanese *are* different. Their instincts *are* different. But in their struggle to catch up to, in Jiro's words, "whatever these outsiders consider to be civilization," the Japanese are making a dedicated effort to balance instinct with the learned responses developed only by international exposure and education. It hasn't been easy, and some of their efforts are way off the mark, but they are working at it.

AMERI-THINK says, "We have to learn more because it's a good thing to do."

JAPAN-THINK says, "We have to learn more in order to survive."

Watch out.

20

· · ·

QUALITY OF LIFE

There are pros and cons to life anywhere. "We have great herring," says the man in Point Barrow, Alaska. "It doesn't rain enough," says the man on Waikiki Beach. "No pollution," says the citizen of Casper, Wyoming. "Broadway's dead," says Manhattan's denizen.

There are good and bad things, to Americans and Japanese, about living in America and living in Japan. But the lists don't match.

· Japanese in America ·

GOOD

1. Space—one can practice golf swings, park two cars, and play catch with the children on one's own property.
2. Fruit can be purchased without the necessity of taking out a bank loan.

3. Blue suits, white shirts, and neckties are not required on Saturday mornings.
4. Kitchens are large enough to cook a meal for the equivalent of the population of Pittsburgh.
5. A round of golf does not require leaving the office or home at midday, twenty-four hours before tee time.
6. It is usually not necessary to wait in line for (A) a public telephone, (B) a public toilet, (C) a public parking lot, (D) a public escalator, and (E) entrance or exit of a public building.
7. It is possible to actually drive an automobile at the speed limit.
8. Restaurants serve the kind of "Japanese" food one only gets to read about in books.
9. If social rules have been violated, no one starts an ostracism movement the next day.
10. Booze is cheap.

· Americans in Japan ·

GOOD

1. The international schools are better than the local schools at home.
2. Taxicabs are all over the place, and will even pick you up in your living room.
3. Random crimes of violence are about as common as colliding planets.
4. Tokyo is actually a huge, walk-through restaurant, and the international food is often better than anything produced in the native country.
5. Titillation abounds.
6. If you suddenly discover you don't have it, there's a vending machine for it.

7. National holidays, snow days, rain days, festival days, and recreation days regularly pop up every couple of weeks.
8. Walking two blocks in any direction is as entertaining as a night at the opera, a day at the circus, a double feature, and a Marx Brothers movie.
9. If social rules have been violated, no one starts an ostracism movement the next day.
10. Walking two blocks in any direction is cheap.

· Japanese in America ·

BAD

1. It's so lonely. Saturday afternoon crowds in a shopping center may only be four or five thousand people.
2. Going into an American restaurant is a continual embarrassment. Only Napoleon's army could finish what they serve to a family of four.
3. Nothing happens on Tuesday nights.
4. The invigorating challenge of commutation is missing.
5. Going out for a walk after dark can be a life-or-death venture.
6. Restaurants don't serve *real* Japanese food.
7. Neither my company, friends, relatives, or personal acquaintances had anything to do with purchasing Rockefeller Center.
8. Obtaining medical treatment is more expensive than buying fruit in Japan.
9. If social rules have been violated, (ssshhh) no one cares.
10. The day will come when the transfer back to Japan is overdue.

· Americans in Japan ·

BAD

1. Getting away from it all is impossible. "It all" is everywhere.
2. Ordering things like "ballet slippers for a doll" is not easy anywhere, but discussing the matter with a shopkeeper accustomed to thinking of language as being a sequence of pictures is particularly frustrating.*
3. Going from point A to point B—wherever.
4. Becoming adjusted to paying the same for breakfast as the cost of a pair of Florsheim shoes.
5. Knowing that no matter how many meetings one attends in Japan, one will never become a member of the club.
6. Seeking medical care for things like a severed jugular and being required to wait in line at the hospital while visitors with hangnails, tired and scratchy eyes, and stubbed toes get to see the one doctor on duty because they were there first.
7. Making reservations to go to the movies.
8. Not finding a pair of slippers in the entire nation that fits.

*Your author, commissioned for domestic chores, once attempted to purchase a dehumidifier. Spotting a *humidifier* in a store, your author began negotiations with the kindly shopkeeper. Indicating that the humidifier was clearly *emitting* humidity—steam was shooting out the nozzle—it seemed logical to graphically demonstrate the characteristics of a machine *retracting* humidity. It only took several minutes of pointing to the nozzle and making sucking gestures and noises before the light dawned. The shopkeeper led your author out of the store, around the corner, across the street, and under the elevated railway tracks. He then pointed proudly to . . . a Japanese noodle shop. (Noodles are slurped in Japan.)

9. Being required to explain all jokes. ("It's not important *what* the traveling salesman was selling, you see, when he asked the farmer if he could spend the night . . .")

10. The day will come when the transfer back to America is overdue.

Tokyo is paradise for someone accustomed to city living and the convenient amenities that are available around every corner. It is not the place for claustrophobics or people who think that "going somewhere" means getting into a car. As is the case in all the great cities of the world, the trick is to reduce it to a livable size. Frequenting the same shops, stores, and service facilities makes one a regular customer, and the reception becomes the same as that in Main Street America.

America is paradise for those with the feeling of having been hemmed in forever. "Room to swing a cat" is sheer luxury to anyone fed up with wondering if it's their own telephone ringing or that of the neighbor next door. More Americans and Japanese are discovering every year the attractions of brief living spells in each country, and this will contribute more to "international understanding" than the study of any textbook. (Is that the phone ringing?)

21
. . .

SUMO

Picture this:

Two big fat guys—wearing next to nothing—waddle up to a three-foot-high pile of packed clay. The crowd screams in anticipation.

The fat guys mount (meaning climb) the pile of clay, which happens to be flat on top. With the grace and magnificence of Ringling Brothers elephants on hind legs, the fat guys go through a hand-clapping, foot-stomping routine that brings the crowd to the brink of hysteria.

Tension builds as the fat guys step into a fifteen-foot circle described by a straw rope partially buried in the clay. They face each other at a distance of five feet, squat on their haunches, and slowly roll forward into four-point stances with their fists on the ground. They glower at each other, faces inches apart, and the crowd goes wild. Shouts of the names of the fat guys rattle the rafters.

Suddenly, the fat guys stand and retreat to opposite sides

of the circle. Anticlimax. The roar of the crowd, like the trough between waves, settles to a smooth and throaty rumble.

Aides to the fat guys provide water in long-handled wooden ladles. The water is not swallowed—it is spit on the ground. Aides also supply the fat guys with towels, which are used for wiping underarms and faces (in that order, by the way).

After perhaps a half minute of this, each fat guy grabs a handful of salt, turns and faces his opponent across the circle, and throws the salt into the air. As the fat guys enter the circle again, the rumble from the crowd becomes again a roar. Some spectators stand and shout the names of their favorites.

The squatting and glowering is repeated. A referee in kimono and pointed hat yells encouragement to the fat guys. As they roll forward into their four-point stances, little things become apparent. What seemed to be fat now ripples with muscle. Definitions of power are obvious in arms, shoulders, backs, and legs. Their faces are strained, and veins appear on foreheads, necks, and ankles. Face-to-face, they are breathing each other's air. The crowd is going bananas.

Again a period of anticlimax as the men stand and return to opposite sides of the circle. The ablution and salt routine is repeated, but the trough between waves of sound in the arena is shorter. In fact by the third or fourth anticlimax, the roar is constant, and earsplitting. Champions in sumo become champions very simply. Throughout their careers, they win more fights than anybody else. They are the strongest, toughest men in the country. Period.

The moment of combat occurs when the crowd has reached the very edge of mass orgasm and the wrestlers have psyched themselves to the point of naked savagery. There is a second's pause, and then two very large, powerful men smash head-on into each other. At anywhere between three hundred and four hundred pounds apiece, the men collide with a force that can be *felt* at the very back row of the arena. The burst of energy required at the outset is that of a sprinter coming off the blocks, the power required is that of a weight-lifter, the balance required is that of a ballet dancer, and for the fights that go beyond a minute, the endurance required is that of a marathoner. To win, one merely throws the other man out of the circle, or causes the other man to touch the clay with anything but the soles of his bare feet. The fight, which may last only seconds, is the maximum of violence compressed into the minimum of time. Winners are national heroes and become millionaires, losers slip down the ranks into oblivion. They do this kind of thing fifteen days in a row, six times a year. And there is no injury reserve list.

Sumo is more than a "sport" in Japan. Sports are games or contests with rules established to make the events more fun, more equal, or more interesting to the spectator and participant. Baseball teams can only have nine players on the field at once—the volley ball net must be the same height for all games. Even boxing, a basic and primal "sport," has rules and regulations to protect the fighters—protective gloves, headgear for amateurs, mandatory rest periods, and proscribed weight limits.

In all cases, the games and contests making up "sports" are nothing more than what they are—games and contests. There is nothing particularly mystical about Carl Lewis trying to beat Ben Johnson to the finish line one hundred meters away. (There may be other issues involved, but they're not mystical.)

Sumo, however, is a physical contest wrapped inside a religious rite. And every aspect of the event is a ritual that has remained essentially unchanged for over *one thousand years*. It is not only the oldest continuously practiced "sport" in the world; it's also the only religious one.

The elaborate process of stomping the earth (from a position with one leg held high above the head) is to summon the "gods" or spirits from the underworld and inform them a "holy" contest is about to begin. Clapping the hands summons the "gods" or spirits from the air. (At one point in the hand-clapping routine, the palms are shown to the opponent—to indicate that no secret weapons are concealed. That sounds pretty "sporting" to your author.)

Throwing salt into the ring is a symbolic purification of the combat ground; rinsing the mouth with water is a symbolic purification of the inner man.

At the conclusion of the bout, the loser climbs back into the ring and ceremoniously bows to the winner—a man the "gods" favored on that particular day. The referee, in kimono and pointed hat, symbolizes a Shinto priest. (Before everyone begins squirming in their seats over the current relevance of these symbolic actions, imagine being an unknowing Japanese and reading about the significance of raising the Host during consecration at a Catholic Mass, or the significance of reading the Haggadah at the Seder ceremonial dinner on the first night of Passover.)

Tournament winners are showered with trophies and prizes, but the one prize of most importance is a sack of rice—the time-honored staple of the nation and the most significant traditional unit of value. (The role of rice in Shintoism and national consciousness is reflected in the enthronement ceremonies of emperors. A new emperor plants new rice from different parts of the nation, symbolizing ongoing life and continuity. The ceremony is no more or less significant than the President of the United States taking the oath of office on a Bible. Keep that in mind as talks continue with Japan over their rice import quotas.)

In addition to the religious implications involved in sumo, there are also several unique aspects regarding participation in the activity. No other "sport" requires participants to adhere to a strict code of conduct and ethics like that demanded of sumoists. The athletes adopt a life-style removed and separate from the common citizen. The preseason training camp rigors in the NFL approach that life-style—dormitory living, training tables, and twenty-four-hour interaction preparing for the season. But once the season begins, an American football player returns to the more normal existence of life with the family in the suburbs. Off-season life is not regulated by mandates of the teams or leagues, and maintaining physical conditioning is a personal responsibility.

Sumo wrestlers, on the other hand, spend their entire careers in a training-camp existence. Not only do they work continually on the techniques of their "sport"; they also give up their personal identity along the way. They assume names given them by their masters and enter a regimen strictly adhering to seniority ranking. "Those who have gone before," not meritocracy, determine who waits on whom. Youngsters entering the program are stripped to the skin and rebuilt both spiritually and physically. Upon retirement, wrestlers "return" the sumo names given them by their masters, but they do not go back to their original names. (The person with the original name no longer exists.) Instead, the ex-wrestler takes an entirely new name that will suit him for the rest of his life.

A fascinating sidebar to the world of sumo is the fact that unlike all other Japanese "sports," there are no restrictions on non-Japanese participation. (Professional baseball in Japan, for example, only allows three foreigners on the roster of each team, with only two of them activated at any one time.) Why would sumo permit it? Two Hawaiians have in recent years risen to the rarified upper ranks. The answer is simple. Once someone has gone through the apprentice period, and accepted a life-style that strips one to the skin for rebuilding, what emerges is . . . a sumo wrestler.

One hesitates to make trite comparisons and to accept "easy" analogies (rice-culture versus hunter-gatherer primitive societies). But the fact remains: all that sumo stands for—and the actual bout in the arena is only part of it—is instinctively respected and admired by the Japanese. Complete and absolute dedication to the cause, submission of individual concerns to an overall structure, spiritual and physical sacrifice under the direction of elders, and acknowledgment of tradition and the quasi-religious "wisdom of the ages" make one a very solid citizen indeed. It's what corporations attempt to instill in employees during orientation programs and "freshman" discipline training camps. ("Mitsubishi Heavy Industries, Steel Exporting Division, Company Two Marketing Department, Assistant Section Chief Watanabe is my name.") The one big difference is that corporate employees get to keep at least part of their names upon retirement.

Another interesting sidebar to the sumo scene is the fact that thirty years ago an American publicist for an American airline company began giving out a massive trophy to sumo tournament champions. Six times a year he would show up in a formal kimono, reel off a presentation speech in semi-adequate Japanese, and present a trophy bigger by about a foot than he is. Crowds would linger after the bouts just to see the man wrestle with both the language and the trophy. Persistence and dedication are admired in Japan. The man was recently presented with one of the Rising Sun awards by the emperor (himself a sumo fan).

That's what it takes in Japan.

Chapter

22

. . .

OBSERVATIONS AND
MISCELLANY

Knowing where to stand in bringing a picture to focus is important. Too far, and only lines and faint daubs of color are discernible. Too close, and we are up against brush strokes, bubbles in paint, and the mechanics of creation. Pity the nearsighted. And the farsighted, too.

Bringing America into focus is difficult for Japanese. Size and diversity inhibit categorization, and create problems in "getting a handle on" people and ideas. Americans are frequently asked by Japanese if they are "typical Americans." This obviously happens more often when the Japanese individual has had limited exposure to Americans, but it is nevertheless a question just under the surface for most Japanese. It is not unusual—in fact, it's quite common—for a Japanese to refer to himself as a "typical" Japanese; it establishes him in the center of things and not out on the fringes of normalcy and conformity. It makes sense to try and pin that down in others as well. When told that there is no such thing as a "typical" American—the range of ethnic, racial, religious, political, philosophical, and economic conditions and circumstances is too broad for simple classification—the Japanese will sadly acknowledge that America can never be fully understood. He may even "sympathize" with the unfortunate American for the hardships he must be enduring in coming from chaos too wide for the frame.

Bringing Japan into focus is not any easier for Americans, but for different reasons. Japan is a "closed" society, and instead of breadth of views there is depth of views. For an outsider to plumb those depths, he must get very close to the painting indeed. One could move to Japan, live with a "typical" family, learn the language, harvest the rice, and attend all the festivals. But then there's the danger of perspective being lost behind brush strokes, bubbles in the paint, and the mechanics of all that goes on.

What all this is leading to is a modest plea that the following observations be accepted as each representing a dash, dot, or daub in the composition of the JAPAN-THINK/ AMERI-THINK picture. (Remember, Claude Monet once demanded that everyone stand nine feet from his paintings.)

JAPAN-THINK knows there is an "age" for everything. Sports cars should not be driven by anyone over the age of twenty-eight, discos should not be frequented by anyone over the age of thirty-five, and the "management" of businesses cannot be handled until at least age fifty. Going on ski trips, eating in "trendy" restaurants, and purchasing popcorn for home consumption is only for people in their mid-thirties or below. A fifty-two-year-old on the ski slopes, for example, is either a foreigner or a "local" from the mountains. A "company president" at age thirty-nine is either a gangster or the son of the owner. Wearing a kimono, unless forced to by job circumstances, is not done by females between the ages of twenty-two and fifty-five. Children under the age of five can go berserk in restaurants and other public places without even a raised eyelid from adults, but the first day of school signals the beginning of a martinet regimen continuing until retirement. Thirty-eight-year-olds cannot go bowling. Only people under twenty-five can drink "light" alcoholic beverages. Unless they are budding professionals, people under thirty-two do not play golf. ("How old *are* you?" a Japanese will ask a colleague derisively who shows up in the office wearing a sport coat and spiffy slacks. Unless people are under twenty-five or over fifty-five, that attire is confined to private parties.) Getting married at forty is best done in secret. The "coming of age" festival, for those turning twenty within the calendar year, is a national holiday.

AMERI-THINK stops counting at thirty, and subtracts a year for every five years over fifty. Anything can be done at any time—it's guaranteed in the Constitution. The fountain of youth, thought originally to be in Florida, probably is. People over thirty-five actually go out dancing. "Hi, there, young man," an insult in Japan, is a compliment in America. Teddy Roosevelt and John F. Kennedy were elected President at the age Japanese salarymen go from section chief to assistant department manager. Retirement is whenever.

JAPAN-THINK recognizes a "season" for everything. "Rainy Season," for example, is when the man on television says it is. If it rains the day before the man on television says it's "Rainy Season," it's just rain. Several years ago it only rained in Japan a half dozen times during the two-month "Rainy Season," but people dragged their umbrellas to work every day. The day after the man on television said "Rainy Season" had ended, it rained. Everyone got soaked to the skin—the umbrellas were home that day. (Going skiing either the day before or the day after "Ski Season" is to be alone with nature.) August 31 can be a damp, overcast day, and beaches will be packed with swarming humanity. September

1 can be 104 degrees in the shade, and not a soul will be in sight. "Swim Season" is over. Air-conditioning goes off in buildings on October 1, the heat goes off April 1. The fact that this can lead to frostbite or heat prostration is the weather's fault—heat and/or air-conditioning must adhere to the rules of "season."

AMERI-THINK, at least a majority of men and a significant minority of women, knows that October is the best month. All major sports "seasons" merge.

JAPAN-THINK accepts the traditional view that the back of a woman's neck is the most attractive part of the body. Kimonos are designed to emphasize the graceful, swanlike look. Tradition and kimono designers notwithstanding, it is virtually impossible to find a man in Japan who will admit to succumbing to the neck's erotic charm. The demands of civilization resulting in covered breasts have diverted attention.

JAPAN-THINK knows that long legs are special. In many cases, long legs are the only things that separate Japanese and non-Japanese in stature. Because of long torsos, most Japanese are taller than most foreigners . . . seated. But, oh, those long legs.

An anecdote is in order here. We are all familiar with racial stereotyping—black guys have a natural sense of rhythm and white guys under six foot five can't stuff the ball. Your author, a white guy, by the way, went to his office in Tokyo one morning with what he thought was an amusing little gag. Like the arrow through Steve Martin's head, your author had a ten-penny nail that appeared to go through his finger. (The little gag comes with a bloody bandage that slips on the finger like a ring.) "I did it hanging a picture," your author explained. (The "hang nail" wordplay sailed over everyone's head, however.) After the "ooohs" and "aaahs," your author announced that the work at hand that morning was too important to interrupt for medical treatment. A half hour later the ambulance arrived. Several days later, when the staff resumed speaking to your author, it was explained that everyone knew the injury was serious, but "it is well-known that foreigners don't feel pain the way we Japanese do." Felt like an ass.

AMERI-THINK has gone through the "real men don't eat quiche" routine. It's a funny catch phrase and it probably applies in many situations. However, Americans know that real men *do* eat quiche and real women *do* eat meatball sandwiches and drink beer from the bottle if the need arises. In Japan, not only are types of food segregated by sex; they can be separated by *age* of sex. The current craze in coffee shops and trendy restaurants is something called "teramiss"—a very creamy cheesecake with chocolate powder sprinkled on top. It apparently is an idea imported from Italy (*tiramisu*). It is a "young lady" delicacy—ordered and eaten *only* by postgraduates up to age thirty-five. Older women would be laughed out of the restaurant if they ordered it; men would be sent to the hospital for extensive tests.

JAPAN-THINK appreciates the "expected" and praises individual effort within the channels. A major criticism of foreigners is that they are always doing the "unexpected."

AMERI-THINK holds that individual creative effort— the light bulb flashing over the head—is both positive and praiseworthy. Dr. Salk formulated the polio vaccine. If that had been in Japan, it would be the Mitsubishi vaccine.

JAPAN-THINK knows that when things get serious, it's better to close in around one's own—like proud flesh on a wound. An employee of your author once "snapped," left his desk in the office, and went to the next-door hotel. There he proceeded to roam throughout the establishment—on the floors with private rooms as well as the restaurants and public areas of the hotel—"preaching" the religious beliefs that had apparently occurred and suddenly overwhelmed him. Your author, in response to a phone call from the hotel's manager, went and got him, convinced the police not to arrest him, contacted the young man's father, and sat soothing him for three hours until arrangements could be made to take him home. Thereafter, despite being in on the escapade from the very beginning, the young man's subsequent fate and state of condition became something "we Japanese will take care of." His work was "covered" by others in the office, and it wasn't until he returned to the office six months later that your author learned he had been "in therapy." It was good to know that he was at least alive.

JAPAN-THINK has times when money—cash—can be touched, and times when it should not. Paying for groceries or a meal in a restaurant is a touchable occasion. Accepting repayment of a loan, or the payment of a gift, is an untouchable occasion. One merely accepts the envelope without looking inside. In addition, one never recounts money in front of someone who has already counted it—bank tellers, store clerks, etc. It's considered to be an insult.

AMERI-THINK makes change by counting *up* to the denomination of currency used in payment. ("Three dollars and sixty-five cents is the charge. Ten plus twenty-five cents and one dollar is your change.")

JAPAN-THINK makes change by mentally subtracting the amount of the charge from the denomination of currency and then counting. ("Three hundred and sixty-five yen is the charge. One thirty-five is your change. Five plus thirty and one hundred is your change.")

AMERI-THINK counts by starting with a closed fist, then raising the index through the little finger, and finally the thumb.

JAPAN-THINK counts by starting with all five fingers extended, and then closing them with the thumb first (and then the index finger through the little finger.) "I'll take two of them," when demonstrated in each country, looks radically different.

AMERI-THINK knows that pointing to oneself means pointing to some area around the middle of the chest—usually near the heart. ("Who, me?")

JAPAN-THINK knows that pointing to oneself means pointing to the tip of the nose. ("Who, me?")

AMERI-THINK has "heart-to-heart" talks.

JAPAN-THINK has "stomach-to-stomach" talks. (Americans cover their chests to protect against a cold; Japanese cover their stomachs.)

JAPAN-THINK knows it's normal to blush when drunk (a missing enzyme in the system does not break down alcohol completely in the stomach—sending the stuff roaring to the capillaries) and giggle when embarrassed.

AMERI-THINK anticipates the opposite.

JAPAN-THINK has a difficult time handling "people who are different." (And to be fair, it is a subject of some concern among thinking Japanese.) A touching documentary made in Japan began with a young boy who had been a "thalidomide baby" born with no arms. His first day of school was filmed by newsreel photographers in the early 1960s. Although kids can be cruel anywhere, this poor boy put up with more abuse than one can imagine in an otherwise civilized society. At first, the other children in the school surrounded him and began questioning him. That's okay. Then someone threw a ball to him. Then someone hit him. The session that first day ended with him head-butting his antagonists merely to keep from being beaten up. His school career was followed down through the years, and it never got much better. The discrimination just got more subtle.

Japanese schoolchildren must follow a strict uniform code without variation. Hair length (plus color and curl), hems, seams, and cuffs are regulated within centimeters. (A kid in

Butte, Montana, who is miffed because school officials won't let him grow a Vandyke beard in eighth grade would be having his fingernails checked in Japan.) A man in his thirties just murdered four of his junior high school classmates. They had taunted him unmercifully during their school days for being "different"—he had been taller than they.

Handicapped people, "different" by definition, are on their own in Japan. One rarely finds facilities accommodating their special needs, and one rarely finds them in the workplace. (Your author, interested in hiring a handicapped woman, met considerable resistance from the other employees. "She won't be able to go on the employee outings.") The "system" very early on implants the idea that "difference" is difficult.

JAPAN-THINK recognizes that once someone is accepted into the group, the acceptance implies complete dedication to the group—for the group's sake. Two people sitting next to each other every day in the office, going to staff meetings together, catching hell from the boss, and getting shit-faced together at company outings will go to each other's weddings, go to funerals of each other's relatives, and do all the things one would expect close friends to do for each other. If one of those people leaves the group, i.e., quits the company, he wouldn't be invited to the other person's wedding even if it was held the next day. (The only exception to this is if the two people had been school classmates. That group rivals in importance the employment group.)

AMERI-THINK knows that a salesman's success depends on the "cold call." ("Hello, I'm Jack, and I have a product designed especially for your needs.") It's what made America great.

JAPAN-THINK welcomes a "cold call" not unlike it would a Scud missile in the living room. Without an "introduction," nothing happens. ("Hello, I am Watanabe whose uncle went to school with your youngest sister's brother-in-law who recommended I call you." "Yes, he, she, they told me.")

AMERI-THINK is into astrology and horoscopes. ("Leaving the house between noon and dusk is very risky, Ronnie, as is accepting overseas calls before Thursday.")

JAPAN-THINK is into character analysis based upon blood type. ("C's are creative flakes and are best paired with benign AB drones.") A major Japanese electronics firm recently staffed one of its research laboratories entirely with B blood types—it's thought they "research" better. The question on blood types appears on the computer questionnaires sent to people enrolling in the marriage matchmaking ventures.

JAPAN-THINK knows that cutting off a cat's tail soon after birth will prevent it from climbing things. (They may be right. Cocker spaniels don't climb things.)

AMERI-THINK places emphasis on winning in sports—"gamers" get the laurels. A ski race means getting to the bottom of the slope before the other guy, a golf match means taking fewer shots at the ball over the course of eighteen holes, a tennis game means blowing more balls past the opponent than he blows past you. *How* that's done is up to the individual and his unique skills or talents.

JAPAN-THINK places emphasis on "form." Tremendous emphasis is placed on getting the swing right, the stance right, and the shots right. (A Japanese champion skier—the only man ever to win an Olympic medal in Alpine skiing from his country—once said he could tell by the sound if a skier on the mountain was Japanese. His boots and skis would click against each other indicating that the parallel "form" was correct. A *real* racer would concentrate on getting to the finish line as fast as possible without falling down—even if the skis were at shoulder-width.) Japanese tennis players have strokes (from perfect positioning and with superb follow-throughs) one would kill for, but no one's ever won a major tournament. And tennis has been played avidly in Japan since the turn of the century. "Form over substance" is an observation of things in Japan made by more than one non-Japanese.

AMERI-THINK is indiscriminate in the "politeness" game. ("Oops, excuse me" is uttered between perfect strangers on the street when brushing into each other.) People in America have even been known to stand and offer a seat to the elderly or infirm on public transportation. Drivers usually accept the rule of alternate progression when cars are forced to merge from two lanes to one.

JAPAN-THINK discriminates in the politeness game. Banging into people on the street, fighting for the first seat on public transportation, and maneuvering one's automobile into every crack of opportunity is accepted and understood. "Wasting" politeness on strangers makes no sense when a great deal of politeness must be extended in personal, face-to-face encounters. The same lady teaching the delicate and refined "tea ceremony" course is the one elbowing and shoving her way to the last seat on the subway. (If the robust young man thirty years her junior gets there first, it's his seat.) The Japanese view is that if everybody stood back and waited, nothing would get done.

JAPAN-THINK laughs when mistakes are made (although it's probably a cover-up for embarrassment). A short-stop will laugh when he boots a simple double-play, strikes out, or misjudges a fly ball. His American counterpart will spit, kick the dirt, or destroy a water cooler in the dugout. Falling down rounding third for home is hilarious in Japan. The same in America could end up being benched for the series.

AMERI-THINK believes in placing blame on the specific offender. If the head of cost accounting is the one charging the Pentagon nine hundred dollars for a screwdriver, he is the one who carries the can. If a lineman for the county mistakenly hooks up a high-power electric line to the telephone wire—thereby blowing out the brains of the next person to call Information—he is the one looking for work the next day. If an oil company's ship captain hits the rocks and spreads gook all over the Alaskan coast, he's the one standing trial.

JAPAN-THINK places blame on the head of the organization in which mistakes occur. The branch manager of a bank found to be fleecing customers to cover his gambling debts will most certainly wind up in hot water (and will never be given comparable authority again), but the president of the bank—who may never have heard the branch manager's name—will "accept all responsibility" and commit ritual suicide by resigning his position. Pressure "to do things right" becomes more than a personal responsibility—it is actually institutional.

AMERI-THINK has developed "no-fault" laws in automobile accidents and divorce proceedings. Although the concept varies from state to state, applications of fault or freedom-from-fault are not objected to in theory—the only considerations are administrative or insurance-related. It is possible in America to be completely innocent, or completely guilty. ("I was just standing here minding my own business.")

JAPAN-THINK knows that everything is in some way interrelated. The "colors" black and white never appear naturally—everything is a shade of gray. In the case of automobile accidents, percentages of accountability are assigned. A driver could be stopped at a light, the car in neutral, and the emergency brake on. A motorcyclist could misjudge things, plow into the side of the car, and flip himself over the top of the vehicle and land on the other side. The chances are that the driver of the car will be blamed for at least a small percentage of the accident—perhaps 5 percent of damages will accrue to him—because (A) his vehicle is larger than the motorcycle, and (B) if he had not been stopped there in the first place the accident would not have occurred. (It is conceivable that a case could be made under B above against a driver vacationing in Hawaii with his car in his own garage at home.)

In the case of <u>divorce</u> in Japan—a phenomenon occurring more frequently as years go by—compromise settlement is also in the gray area. Courts discourage divorce matters from getting that far, and instead encourage negotiations between the families involved and the "go-betweens" who either symbolically or actually arranged the weddings. Rights and wrongs are analyzed in detail, responsibilities are discussed and confirmed, and financial matters are agreed upon on a onetime, lump-sum basis. The relationship is severed, no regular alimony payments ensue, and the only ongoing responsibility is to the children's welfare.

AMERI-THINK is concerned with the pollution problem. It is everybody's concern, and controls are fairly evenly distributed between corporate entities and private citizens. Smokestack laws are more or less in place and prosecution can occur, companies like McDonald's voluntarily stopped selling burgers encased in undissolvable material, and all vehicles are equipped with some kind of antipollution device. At least "awareness" is there.

JAPAN-THINK is also "aware" of the dangers of pollution, but control is a two-step process. Private vehicles have pollution-control devices, they must be checked on a regular basis, and foreign imports must adhere to the strict and slightly different codes. Keep in mind, however, the close cooperation between government and business. The second step in the process has not been taken yet—trucks and buses belch pollutants into the air without control. The hardship of converting to controls, which private citizens are asked to make, is considered to be too much of an economic burden for large companies to make.

JAPAN-THINK places great value in statistics. (Ninety-three percent of Japanese men going to a public bath prefer to sit in the corner nearest to the door.) In a homogeneous society, statistics say something. (Men spend forty-five seconds cleaning their genitals prior to entering the bath whereas women spend less than twenty seconds on the same chore.) When education has been standardized and group participation has been emphasized, the parts *really* become the whole, and vice versa. (Eighty-eight percent of men prefer using the public urinal farthest from the door, yet they prefer to bathe the same machinery at the opposite end of the room.) These things are not made up—the major daily newspapers report the results of surveys almost every day. (Over 90 percent of Japanese people consider themselves to be middle class.) Knowing that one falls into the comfortable majority is satisfying. (Ninety-nine percent of Japanese businessmen in their fifties "feel exhausted.") The statistics themselves are not quite that important. (Over 90 percent of Japanese women would worry about a love affair being discovered by a boyfriend or husband.) What is more interesting is the fact that the surveys are even *conceived.* (Ninety-one percent of Japanese women working in offices believe their breasts are "inadequate.") Or even answered. (Almost 80 percent of Japanese women report that the last thing they wash in their bath is their feet.) One thing we do know for certain. (Seventy-nine percent of Japanese teenagers are certain it's okay to have premarital sex.) Depending upon the structure of the question—remember, we're dealing in a picture language here—results can be surprisingly confounding. (Eighty-seven percent of Japanese men going to a public bath prefer to sit in the corner *farthest away* from the door, repeat, *farthest away* from the door.) Since that answer is diametrically opposed to the answer given in the first example quoted here, either the question was misunderstood one of those two times, or a cultural revolution is under way. (But one can't help picturing a herd of naked men circling the communal pool and wondering which end—nearest or farthest from the door—one is expected to prefer.)

AMERI-THINK considers, depending on the standards and framework of the question, anywhere from 30 to 49 percent of the population to be in a "minority" group.

JAPAN-THINK reckons that if the population of the country is related to a twenty-four-hour day, "minorities" make up one minute and nine seconds. And that number is certain.

AMERI-THINK flat-out knows that the United States consists of 3,608,787 square miles of land and 3,680,114 square miles of land *and* possessions. (Equally precise measurements of coastline also exist.) The *number* of Americans occupying that space is at best an approximation. Depending on whether or not federal census numbers are believed, local numbers are believed, or the theoretically neutral numbers of statisticians are believed, the population is between 230 million and 260 million.

JAPAN-THINK flat-out knows that the population was 123,456,789 on May 30, 1990. (As of the *hour* of this writing, the population of Japan is 123,644,588.) Everyone is registered. But depending on whether or not the national government is believed, Japan Travel Bureau is believed, or the Japan Cartographers Association is believed, the *size* of Japan is anywhere from 141,529 square miles to 149,366 square miles, and the country is composed of either "four main islands and a number of minor islands" or "five main islands and several minor possessions." America has the real estate under control; Japan has the people under control.

AMERI-THINK measures distances between cities and towns from "city limits" to "city limits."

JAPAN-THINK measures distances between cities and towns from arbitrarily selected "city centers" to "city centers." (One can go thirty miles *in* Tokyo until getting *to* Tokyo— an historic area "downtown" called Nihonbashi.)

AMERI-THINK knows that St. Valentine's Day is the time to give lovers and "special friends" little gifts—often chocolate and often from male to female.

JAPAN-THINK knows that St. Valentine's Day is the time for women and women only to buy chocolate and chocolate only for the men in their lives—including *any* male they may remotely come in contact with over the course of the year. In a brilliant marketing ploy, the chocolate industry has supported the new "White Day" practice one month later during which all men receiving chocolate on St. Valentine's Day must reciprocate with an identical gift.

JAPAN-THINK recognizes the fish-scaling knife as being the number-one homicide weapon in the country, followed closely by the baseball bat (aluminum). School authorities are meeting with the baseball bat (aluminum) manufacturers to get "sound dampeners" incorporated into bat construction. This has nothing to do with homicide—instead it has been determined that the "ping" of hitting a baseball with the bats (aluminum) is at such a decibel level that young ears are damaged. (American bats—aluminum—have been tested in Japan and shown to create less noise on contact with the ball, but of course importing them is unthinkable. These are *Japanese* boys playing with them.)

AMERI-THINK admits that American bat (aluminum)

manufacturers have contemplated committing homicide in Japan with their nonadmitted stock in trade.

JAPAN-THINK believes certain foreign products won't work in Japan. Mosquitoes, it is thought, are different, and therefore won't respond to alien repellents. (Skis from overseas were thought at first to be unsuitable for Japanese snow, but the overwhelming popularity of European and American brand "names" made it impossible to keep them out. Now they work in Japanese snow.)

Chapter

23
. . .

IT'S TIME TO RETIRE

As mentioned earlier, in Japan the corporate retirement age of fifty-five was established when the life expectancy of males was around fifty-eight. The life expectancy began rising steadily after the war—it is now the highest in the world—but the figure fifty-five was maintained until only the last few years. (Many companies have increased the age to fifty-seven or fifty-eight, and a few companies have gone to sixty.)

Why such a grudgingly small increase when people are living close to thirty years *after* retirement? The "lifetime employment" practice in Japan bound employers and employees to each other, and from the employer's point of view, personnel costs could be controlled by a regular and scheduled rotation of people between ages twenty-two and fifty-five. Only top officers of companies escaped being replaced in the "body count" figures by cheaper youngsters. The "lifetime employment" practice is beginning to crumble— Japanese salarymen are beginning to consider job changes in d-career—but flexibility in type and length of employment is still limited, and way behind the choices open to an American employee. Top officers of companies can usually work until sixty-five, and then they are hired back as advisers until age 130 or death, whichever occurs first.

AMERI-THINK considers the period after age sixty-five retirement as the "Golden Years"—a time when sailing trips around the world can be scheduled, the ranch house on the golf course can be built, and life can focus on going from one child's house to another to bask in the glow of love and respect from grateful and well-behaved grandchildren. The only problem is keeping in touch with the stockbroker over the management of the pension funds and other bits and pieces of income issuing from several different sources. (The reality of the matter, of course, is that scraping by on a fixed income—with inflation constantly eating into the value of any reserves—is a daily battle. Plus grandchildren aren't as well-behaved as grandchildren used to be.)

JAPAN-THINK knows that retirement at fifty-five means it's time to start the "second career." Retirement benefits are usually paid in a lump sum—regular monthly pension payments are rare. With that capital as a cushion, a fifty-five-year-old will start a small service business of his own and at the same time try to hook on to one of his former company's subsidiaries on a part-time consulting basis. If that is not possible, he will seek employment with a small family-owned business operated by an old school friend or with a former business contact developed and cultivated along the way. There is also the option of working in an administrative capacity for schools, clubs, or social organizations. The advantage a Japanese retiree has is that it is easier to begin the "second career" at fifty-five than at sixty-five. His "Golden Years" also begin at sixty-five—the government "old-age" pension kicks in then—but by that time he has the option of

staying on in the second job or cashing in on wl
two nest eggs.

AMERI-THINK considers retirement to be a time to
slow down, play a few rounds of golf with old cronies, and
generally concentrate on keeping body and soul together and
in reasonably good health. Taking a trip now and then, plus
working up to a regular game of cards a couple of times a
week, is all the exercise one needs, thank you very much.

JAPAN-THINK knows that retirement is to begin a wild
flurry of activity the likes of which was totally unthinkable in
the salaryman's world. There are bicycle-racing clubs, moun-
tain-climbing clubs, marathon-running clubs, and skiing-like-
lunatics-down-the-side-of-an-icy-mountain clubs. Seventy-
year-olds take up hot-air ballooning, cross-country trekking,
and badminton. Eighty-year-olds hold swim meets and volleyball tournaments. For the "elderly" there is the more se-
date game of gateball, a Japanese form of croquet. Dressed
in uniforms of white shoes and pants, with "club" blazers and
matching hats, contestants travel all over the country for
matches and tournaments. There are leagues (*leagues,* mind
you) for teams with players averaging a *minimum* of ninety
years of age!

The problem of housing affects both the Japanese and
American elderly—the transformation from a primarily rural
society to urban life has created major problems in both countries. At least the Americans have more space in homes for
three-generation families. Elbows can be put through the
paper walls in Japanese houses, and in three-generation families they frequently are.

Chapter

24

. . .

WHERE DO WE GO FROM HERE?

As a general statement, it's fair to say there are three basic views of Japan held by Americans.

AMERI-VIEW #1: "Because the culture and history of Japan are so different, it's impossible for an outsider to even begin to understand the intricate machinations of mind and soul that have resulted in today's state of affairs." This view has long been held by Americans who have run up against roadblocks in the pursuit of business or trade with Japan— and the solution traditionally has been to "try harder" to find the cracks and niches where success is permitted. There *have* been some notable successes in the cracks and niches, and these have been pointed to by both sides as evidence that Japan is an open market despite its peculiar customs.

AMERI-VIEW #2: "Japan's postwar successes are less a matter of cultural uniqueness than they are the result of some very basic, hardheaded decisions made by government, political, and business leaders who knew, and still know, exactly what they're doing." This view, a "revisionist" theory of things, is currently in vogue and has brought the analysis of America-Japan relationships to new levels of debate. The view variously holds that the close cooperation of financial institutions and industry, government and financial institutions, workers and industry, or "society" and "establishment" has contrived to knock the underpinnings out from under any and all competition from outsiders standing in the way of success.

AMERI-VIEW #3: "When it gets right down to it, people are people, and competing with Japan is just a matter of working through the issues one by one." This view is held by realists less interested in reflecting upon causes than reveling in results. "Japan had better change its distribution system or we'll put prohibitive tariffs on their products."

It may have occurred to the reader that the best interpretation is one that accepts parts of all three views in interaction with each other, rather than adhering to an exclusive analysis of things.

Japan *is* different. The longest any Americans (other than Amer-Indians) have lived on the North American continent is 350 years. An increasing percentage of Americans have lived in the United States less than one generation. The only "common" aspect of life is the language—which is marginal in some communities—and the general belief that the "American way of life" is preferable to life anywhere else on the globe. These are practical and edifying agents of cohesion, but they don't begin to compare with the "oneness" felt by Japanese. Remember, they are just getting around to "adjusting" the law—to take effect nearly two years from now—which requires fingerprinting of Koreans whose ancestors have lived in Japan for almost a century. The average American and the average Japanese may not know for certain where their great-great-ever-so-great grandfather was living specifically, but at least the Japanese knows that he was living in Japan, speaking Japanese, and trundling off to the shrine on holidays and special occasions during and in between cooperative rice production 1,500 years ago. That's heavy-duty continuity, and with all the hocus-pocus that becomes ritualized in cultural matters over a period of time, reactions, impulses, and instincts become very unique indeed. Make no mistake about it, Japanese are coming from somewhere else.

Is there collusion among big business, government, and financiers? You bet there is. Why not? After being devastated by the war, and not exactly dwelling in a bed of roses in the first place, the average Japanese man on the street willingly gave up any notion of "consumer rights" for the more basic principle of "survival." What's good for Mitsubishi has certainly been very good for Japan. Folks have jobs. And for those who think that "collusion" is bad and should be broken up, try to locate the target. In Japan, the prime minister, the head of the Bank of Japan, and the chairman of Mitsubishi don't sit in one room and carve out fiefdoms and appoint central controllers. The "collusion" is instead indirect—it is a tacit agreement that allows the successful producers to have free rein in matters related to their best interests. This of course makes it very difficult for competition, but Japan has never held that "equal opportunity" is the golden rule. Sumo wrestlers are not classified by weight. If a small guy, or small company, comes along and whips the grand champion—fine. But remember, he had no special help along the way, and he fights on terms dictated by the big and powerful. His tools are competitiveness and price, his enemy is size and strength. Other than that, there is no discrimination. As the strong get stronger, markets become increasingly dominated.

Despite the above, people *are* people. Taken out of the "systems" and cultural frameworks within which everyone operates, the basic issues of life, happiness, health, security, and love are standard across-the-board concerns of mankind. Of particular interest is the fact that tens of thousands of Japanese are vitally concerned about the rifts that have developed between America and Japan. They recognize the problem, and would do anything in their power to work toward solutions. Many of the people are those who have had exposure abroad—generally the better-educated and more thoughtful individuals—but a great number are people running the corner grocery stores who, on their own, have formed opinions about the state of world affairs.

> AMERI-THINK: "Play by the rules, dammit, or there'll be hell to pay."
> JAPAN-THINK: "We *are* playing by the rules, dammit, but they're *our* rules."
> AMERI-THINK: "*Your* rules? Why should we play by your rules?"
> JAPAN-THINK: "You took the words out of our mouths."

Japanese and Americans each do what they know best. "Knowing" things, however, is shaped by experience. Americans with any experience in Japan know that the black-and-white distinction is never as clear as that depicted in texts. Although "frontal assaults" are preferred by Americans and employed every step of the way, there is also the real awareness that to get anything accomplished one must romance ministry officials, develop relationships for introductions, entertain powerful characters in various dens of iniquity, and be prepared to return "favors" for "favors" in ways head office accountants and Internal Revenue Service civil servants will never fully appreciate. ("Entertainment charges of $2,000 last night? That was, ah, oh, yeah, 'health club' membership fees.")
Japanese with any experience in America innately know

that black and white do not exist. "Frontal assaults" will be
attempted because that's the way things are done in America,
but they'll also attempt the things *they* believe are most effective—romancing government officials, developing relationships for introductions, entertaining powerful characters
in various dens of iniquity, and being prepared to return
"favors" for "favors" (in ways Japanese tax people *do* understand). To be shocked and horrified by this, and to view this
as another "sneak attack," is to be woefully naïve. That's
business, folks. If a carpet merchant discovers that accompanying blow jobs are required to move the merchandise,
accompanying blow jobs will be arranged.

AMERI-THINK: "The Japanese are buying up
America."
JAPAN-THINK: "The Hotel Okura is packed with
carpetbaggers from America, and we've had to hire
and staff entire departments to sift through 'investment opportunities' offered to us. The problem is not
what to buy, but what *not* to buy."

Are there solutions to the problems facing America in its
relationship with Japan—problems involving hundreds of
millions of dollars in trade imbalances? There are solutions,
perhaps not perfect ones and certainly not ones that will
reverse trends tomorrow morning, but they represent the
course that must be taken.

• • •

Words are fine, but hours, days, months, and years can
be spent puzzling over nuances (color-blind and horny—one
teeny-tiny vowel). Careers are made and spent over inter-
pretations. Will a trade representative be able to "talk" the
other side into doing what decades of others have tried to

"talk" their way through? Un-bloody-likely. America is Japan's most important market, and every man, woman, and child in Japan knows that. Not only are marketing projections and training programs geared to the American market; investments in America now help support Japan's economy. From the Japanese point of view, "talks" can go on forever, or at least as long as the Americans are willing to sit around the table and drink green tea. A fish to the jumping dolphin here, a peanut to the performing elephant there, and everything's right with the world.

"Open markets" is a principle that must be maintained, and no one disagrees with that. But *ban* (meaning *ban*) Japanese automobile exports to America for six months or until plans are made to accommodate equal reciprocal arrangements, and the speed with which adjustments are made will make heads swim. Japan is nothing if not pragmatic (no pubic hair and no organs of either kind). What will they do, replace America with the Singaporean market? In dealing with a country ruled primarily by bureaucracy (and not the political prime-minister-of-the-moment smiling on visits to the oval office), a *reason* must be given for radical change. The gallons of green tea consumed by negotiators are not enough. An attack on the corporate pocketbook is. And *that* is a rule completely understandable. The game is hardball, not softball. (Nothing personal, mind you.)

• • •

An American company should not even *be* in Japan unless it is willing to send its most talented executives to the marketplace. Japan ain't Jakarta. To put "career path" executives in Tokyo who are merely interested in leveraging the Japan Experience into a promotion from the Kansas City branch to the East Orange region is dumb. (Words, your author is reluctant to admit when discussing this subject, fail.)

Japan *is* made up of people at least willing to listen to ideas and concepts beyond those slammed into their heads by education and the "system." There is a basic admiration for "things American"—not because Japan will ever become "Americanized" in the foreseeable future, but because America has provided the country with countless things that can be adapted to the "Japanese way." (If Japan did not become "Americanized" during Emperor Meiji's heyday, and later during the Occupation, there's no reason to believe that the current popularity of Kentucky Fried Chicken and Levi's is going to swing it now.) But alumni groups of those that have studied or worked abroad, employees of international corporations, and reflective members of the establishment at various levels *are* interested in debate and discussion leading at least to a better understanding of the issues that will be affecting America-Japan relations in the years to come.

Japan will not become American. America will not become Japanese. But the fortunes of the peoples are intertwined. And "understanding," despite the pressures of economics, has never been greater.

"Are you worried, Jiro?"
"Of course I'm worried. We may never be able to figure them out."

"But *really* whaddya think, Jake?"
"We may be getting in over our heads. We can't even tell what they're thinking."

FOR THE BEST IN PAPERBACKS, LOOK FOR THE

In every corner of the world, on every subject under the sun, Penguin represents quality and variety—the very best in publishing today.

For complete information about books available from Penguin—including Pelicans, Puffins, Peregrines, and Penguin Classics—and how to order them, write to us at the appropriate address below. Please note that for copyright reasons the selection of books varies from country to country.

In the United Kingdom: For a complete list of books available from Penguin in the U.K., please write to *Dept E.P., Penguin Books Ltd, Harmondsworth, Middlesex, UB7 0DA*.

In the United States: For a complete list of books available from Penguin in the U.S., please write to *Dept BA, Penguin*, Box 120, Bergenfield, New Jersey 07621-0120.

In Canada: For a complete list of books available from Penguin in Canada, please write to *Penguin Books Canada Ltd, 10 Alcorn Avenue, Suite 300, Toronto, Ontario, Canada M4V 3B2*.

In Australia: For a complete list of books available from Penguin in Australia, please write to the *Marketing Department, Penguin Books Ltd, P.O. Box 257, Ringwood, Victoria 3134*.

In New Zealand: For a complete list of books available from Penguin in New Zealand, please write to the *Marketing Department, Penguin Books (NZ) Ltd, Private Bag, Takapuna, Auckland 9*.

In India: For a complete list of books available from Penguin, please write to *Penguin Overseas Ltd, 706 Eros Apartments, 56 Nehru Place, New Delhi. 110019*.

In Holland: For a complete list of books available from Penguin in Holland, please write to *Penguin Books Nederland B.V., Postbus 195, NL-1380AD Weesp, Netherlands*.

In Germany: For a complete list of books available from Penguin, please write to *Penguin Books Ltd, Friedrichstrasse 10-12, D-6000 Frankfurt Main 1, Federal Republic of Germany*.

In Spain: For a complete list of books available from Penguin in Spain, please write to *Longman, Penguin España, Calle San Nicolas 15, E-28013 Madrid, Spain*.

In Japan: For a complete list of books available from Penguin in Japan, please write to *Longman Penguin Japan Co Ltd, Yamaguchi Building, 2-12-9 Kanda Jimbocho, Chiyoda-Ku, Tokyo 101, Japan*.

FOR THE BEST IN PAPERBACKS, LOOK FOR THE

Other business books available from Penguin:

☐ **TAKEOVER**
Moira Johnston

Focusing on three of the biggest takeover battles of the 1980s—Carl Icahn's bid for TWA, T. Boone Pickens' failed quest for Unocal, and Sir James Goldsmith's triumph over Crown Zellerbach—*Takeover* spotlights the new Wall Street Warriors.

"A brilliantly reported examination of the takeover wars that are restructuring U.S. industry"—*Business Week*
                    418 pages   ISBN: 0-14-010505-0

☐ **GETTING TO YES**
Negotiating Agreement Without Giving In
Roger Fisher and William Ury

Based on studies conducted by the Harvard Negotiation Project, this straightforward how-to presents a universally applicable method for negotiating personal and professional disputes without getting taken and without getting nasty.

"By far the best thing I've ever read about negotiation"—John Kenneth Galbraith   *162 pages   ISBN: 0-14-006534-2*

FOR THE BEST IN PAPERBACKS, LOOK FOR THE

☐ **THE TAO JONES AVERAGES**
A Guide to Whole-Brained Investing
Bennett W. Goodspeed

Mixing the wisdom of the Taoist sages with the Wall Street savvy of seasoned investors, Bennett W. Goodspeed shows how to use both hemispheres of your brain to anticipate market fluctuations and achieve greater financial returns.

"Illuminating and refreshing"—*Barron's*
156 pages   ISBN: 0-14-007368-X

☐ **ALL AMERICA'S REAL ESTATE BOOK**
Everyone's Guide to Buying, Selling, Renting, and Investing
Carolyn Janik and Ruth Rejnis

Covering every aspect of the real estate marketplace, this extraordinary guide contains the up-to-date facts and down-to-earth advice needed to buy, sell, or lease property.

"Exhaustively handles the many aspects of real estate in a calm but interesting way."—*Christian Science Monitor*
852 pages   ISBN: 0-14-009416-4

☐ **GETTING YOURS**
The Complete Guide to Government Money
Matthew Lesko

This national best-seller from the author of *Information U.S.A.* is the key to financing any endeavor, from a farm to a college education, with the help of federal and state government funds.

"Lesko gives you hundreds of ways to get dollars and other favors from the federal government."—*USA Today*
368 pages   ISBN: 0-14-046760-2

☐ **SELLING MONEY**
S.C. Gwynne

A young banker's account of the great international lending boom, *Selling Money* elucidates the workings of the world of international finance and the startling history of the great debt crisis.

"Bids fair to do for international lending what *Funny Money* did for the collapse of the Penn Square Bank."—*The New York Times Book Review*
182 pages   ISBN: 0-14-010282-5